Smoke
to See By

Knowing Nature in Northern Appalachia

BEN MOYER

CATAMOUNT
PRESS

an imprint of Sunbury Press, Inc.
Mechanicsburg, PA USA

CATAMOUNT
PRESS

an imprint of Sunbury Press, Inc.
Mechanicsburg, PA USA

For information about special discounts for bulk purchases, please contact Sunbury Press Orders Dept. at (855) 338-8359 or orders@sunburypress.com.

To request one of our authors for speaking engagements or book signings, please contact Sunbury Press Publicity Dept. at publicity@sunburypress.com.

FIRST CATAMOUNT PRESS EDITION: March 2023

Set in Adobe Garamond | Interior design by Crystal Devine | Cover by Lawrence Knorr | Edited by Lawrence Knorr.

Publisher's Cataloging-in-Publication Data
Names: Moyer, Ben, author.
Title: Smoke to see by : knowing nature in northern Appalachia / Ben Moyer.
Description: First trade paperback edition. | Mechanicsburg, PA : Catamount Press, 2023.
Summary: *Smoke to See By* is a collection of 21 essays and stories, many never before published, written by award-winning essayist and columnist Ben Moyer. The collection tracks the writer's quest for intimate knowledge of, and personal connection to, the natural features of his home region, the foothills and ridges of Northern Appalachia.
Identifiers: ISBN : 979-8-88819-093-7 (softcover) | ISBN : 979-8-88819-094-4 (ePub).
Subjects: NATURE / Regional | LITERARY COLLECTIONS / Essays | SPORTS & RECREATION / Fishing.

Product of the United States of America
0 1 1 2 3 5 8 13 21 34 55

Continue the Enlightenment!

For

Kathy, Colleen, Aaron, Safari, Max, Julie, and Rich

Contents

Acknowledgments

The author wishes to acknowledge and thank *Pittsburgh Quarterly*, initial publisher of *Surviving Summit Mountain*; *Blackberry, The Humblest Jewel*; and *Memoirs of a Quehanna Chief.* The same acknowledgement and appreciation are due Northern Appalachia Review, initial publisher of *Fraxinus Lost, Dunbar Creek; Perception and Place*, and *Nothing Spectacular*; to *Gray's Sporting Journal*, initial publisher of *Smoke to See By*, to *Pennsylvania Outdoor News*, initial publisher of *Summer's Upstream Allure*, to *Pennsylvania Game News*, initial publisher of *Red Oak, White Oak*; *Under Plover's Wings, Kettles of Grace, Encountering 'cats, Known to Crows*, and *Afterglow*, and to *Uniontown Herald Standard*, initial publisher of a different version of *Tea for Two*.

Introduction

The concept of place has always felt important to me. I like to know *where* I am and to sense the context of that place in relation to features such as a mountain range or coastline or within a watershed, and to know how that place fits within artificial manmade borders.

While *place* seems to be declining in importance in modern life (Cell phone numbers are geographically arbitrary, and how often do you see a physical address displayed now in advertisements?), I've kept a "landline" telephone number because that three-digit code—329—identifies me as living within a particular swath of landscape, roughly 60 miles square. When someone tells a story, I'll interrupt to ask where this happened, craving more geographic detail than the teller was prepared, or felt was relevant to share. Details about place and setting lend texture to a story that deepens meaning.

An unavoidable extension of that interest in place is my belief that it is satisfying, meaningful, and of value to know things about the natural character of the place where one lives—its climate, weather, vegetation, topography, native creatures, and the history of our interaction with those elements. Knowledge of one's *place* enhances life in the way details of setting add texture to stories. Knowledge engenders affinity. So, knowledge may also enable the future to be more deferential toward the natural underpinnings of place than our past.

Naming *my place* is not difficult. I am from, and of, the hilly and modestly mountainous southwestern corner of Pennsylvania, where the western limits of the northeast-to-southwest-slanting Allegheny Mountains stand above a maze of hills to their west, where seasons are distinct and dependable and where, due to past and present climate, drainage patterns and topography, a marvelous convergence of native vegetation and wildlife blends from the four points of the compass. One of the densest networks of flowing waters—streams and rivers—on Earth grace these uplands, originally, and still in places, cold and clear. Here, despite its proximity to urban centers and its fevered industrial history, vestiges of the unsettled Appalachian region remain. For the fortunate, as I have been, here it is not difficult to access, participate in, relate to, and grow to know these varied facets of *place*. Most of this region is still rural, some family connections to land remain intact, and ample public tracts of forest and parkland welcome entry by all who know about their existence and are willing to respect their rules of use.

Coming to know some things about *my place*, I was most fortunate that my father, all my uncles, and most of our family's neighbors and friends hunted and fished. They took me with them to the woods, fields, and streams when I was too young to carry a gun or cast a line but could follow along. Soon, owing to those early outings, fishing and hunting, to me, felt like something more than a diversion or pastime, and still do. These pursuits felt like a way to reach toward something profound and fundamental, something authentic that no other person could manufacture, make, or sell. I was helped, unconsciously, I think, in sensing this by my mentors' behavior in the woods, especially my father's, who never displayed disrespect toward or dominion over the deer and grouse we killed or the trout we caught and creeled. Hunting and fishing were our default ways to *be* in what remained of the natural place where we found ourselves on the Earth, and hunting and fishing steered me toward curiosity for and awareness of nature beyond the game that was legal to take by gun or rod.

The stories, narratives, and accounts within this book are not *about* hunting and fishing, though some are set there, but all came out of an awareness or at least from my frequent attempts toward awareness of the larger natural realm, which is always elusive, which hunting and fishing first catalyzed. Still, knowing facts may be less important than striving to know, which explains why humans write, paint, carve, cook, or still fish in economies where it's economically redundant.

All places yet blessed with a semblance of their natural distinctiveness are worthy of notice, contemplation and, especially, sharing within humility. This is my attempt from here.

In Our Place

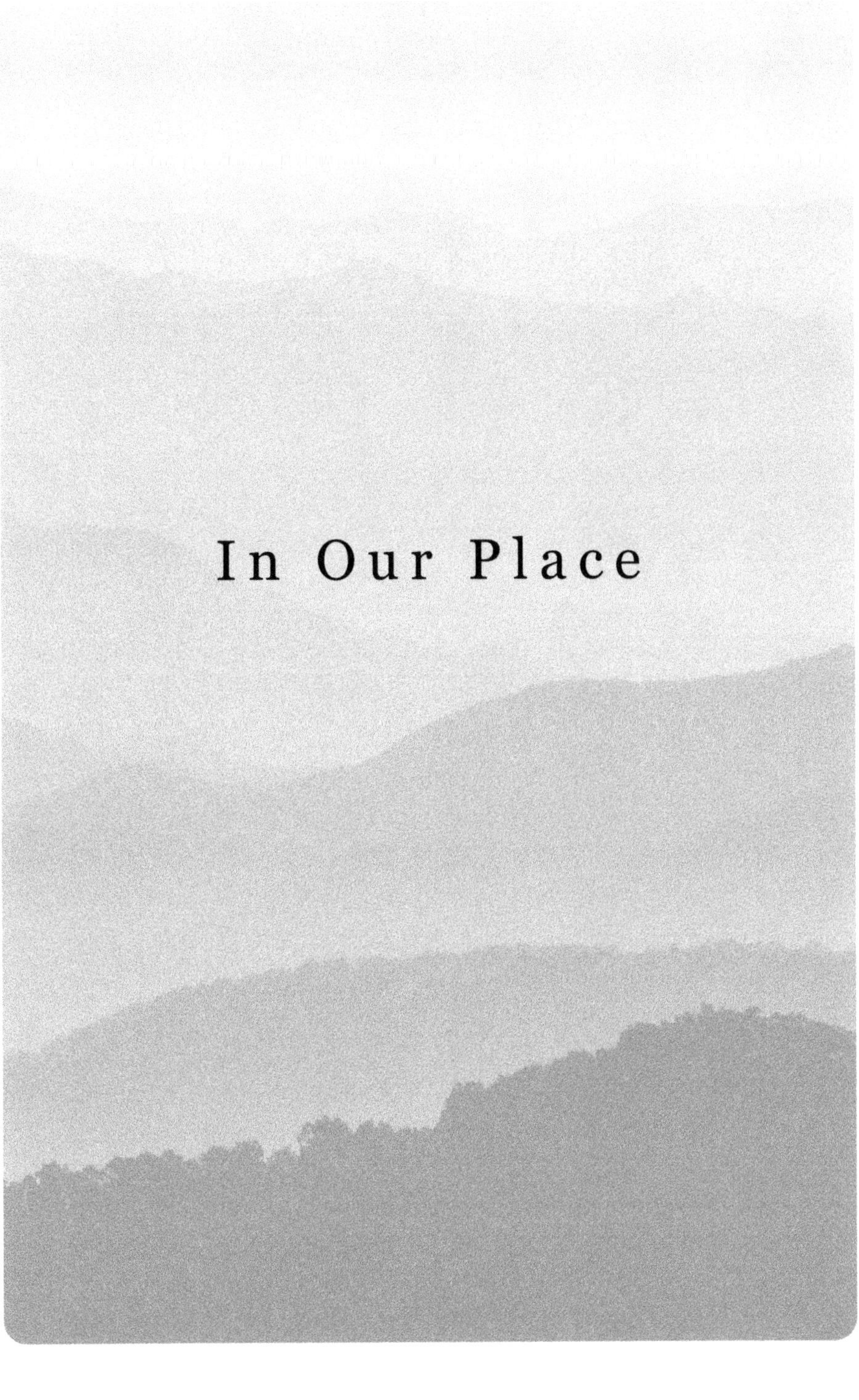

Nothing Spectacular

Few who have traveled much would call the hills of Greene County, Pennsylvania, "spectacular." Even by Appalachian scale, they are modest rounded mounds. Their folds conceal no caverns or cataracts. Their most rugged features are scattered stony outcrops. Snow never blanches their summits unless it covers the whole scene. While predictably southwest-to-northeast-bearing ridges define much of Pennsylvania's upland topography, Greene County, wedged by West Virginia in the state's southwest corner, is a random morass of hollow and hill. Here, you cannot guide yourself by the lay of the hills. They wander.

Streams here run to the Monongahela River in eastern Greene and directly to the Ohio in the west. But there's no sharp boundary between those basins, no crest where you know you have crossed a divide. Driving west across the county from the "Mon" on Rte. 21, you grow accustomed to all roadside streams opposing your progress, flowing back toward the way you came. Somewhere past Waynesburg, though, you'll suddenly note that the little creek below the road is tracking your course, sliding west toward the Ohio out of some wrinkle in the hills, trailing you now like a sniffing predator that's snuck up from behind. Where hills wander, streams behave the same, sluggish, unspectacular as the knobs they drain.

A widely traveled visitor's first sight of Greene County, or much of the Alleghenies' western foothills, might understandably result in such a mundane impression. But that would be a limiting view, informed by screen shots and televised images of "spectacular" places elsewhere—alpine peaks, tempestuous coasts, lush tropical beaches. My way of thinking about landscapes holds that "spectacular" is a glib and artificial idea, risen out of casual admiration of famous locations. Through that lens, there is no such thing as "spectacular," for to hail one place as "spectacular" risks missing the remarkable elsewhere.

For example, many places in the American West are extolled as "spectacular." The West's high mountain vastness, austere deserts, and yawning canyons have been pictured and revered as archetypes of the raw North American continent. Such adulation, though, misses the truth that all landscapes contain, or did contain, their own unique, time-fitted processes, qualities, and elements that make or made them function as they must.

The "spectacular" West, as we see it now, is an accident of history, resulting from eastern North America's being "discovered," explored, settled, and subjugated earlier than the West, so that much of what we might have seen as spectacular here was gone before we knew to miss it.

Had the continent been settled in reverse, from west to east, and had a conservation ethic evolved before civilization reached the unequaled Appalachian hardwood forest, preserving vast tracts in their natural state in public ownership, we would today celebrate "spectacular" old-growth American chestnut, tulip poplar, and oak stands on Greene County hills in the same way we exalt the Grand Canyon itself. Our experience with woodland here, cut over and regrown multiple times, scourged by invasive plants, does not prepare us even to imagine the forest that cloaked these hills, the forest they are capable of hosting. Were we somehow able to visit that native forest, to follow a trail into its depth, we would find ourselves awed, hushed within the native spectacle of this place.

We cannot, of course, walk such a trail. Still, acknowledging what was once here, what could, theoretically, be here again, keeps us open to note and revere the spectacular that remains, and it does remain.

A report of forest resources produced by the U. S. Forest Service states that in 1960, 19 percent of Greene County's surface was covered by woodland. Today, reverting woods on abandoned farm and pastureland cover about 60 percent of the county, and it's likely that the 1960 stat already reflected an upswing in forest reversion. The low point in forest cover, perhaps less than 10 percent, probably came around the turn of the 20th century.

Greene County was sheep and beef country then, an expanse of wrinkled pasture, and still was in 1960. Sheep ranged as white clumps over the knobs and slopes, surrounded by scattered stragglers. Red and black beef cows grazed the bottoms. Dark lines also networked the hills, a grid of big, spreading oaks, beeches, and sugar maples, gigantic even then, left uncut by herders to mark boundaries between their fields. Many of those boundary giants are still there but less conspicuous now, masked among reverting growth that sprang up as hill country sheep farmers died off or gave up.

Walking these woods, searching for morels in spring, or hunting a deer in the fall, you'll know the old trees when you come up under them. Their bulk and reach are so immense that they could be a different species from the saw-timber offspring around them. Their presence will arrest, press you to linger.

A line of gigantic oaks crowns a ridge crest where I have hunted deer over many seasons. The oaks were massive when I first saw them as an excited boy. I know they have grown through the ensuing decades, but any change in their height, girth and spread is imperceptible to me. I see them not so much as individual trees but as the commanding essence of the setting there. They are constants. Sometimes one of the oaks will shed a branch, which falls to ground and dwarfs all surrounding upstarts.

I have often climbed to the oaks in mid-winter, after all the deer seasons, because it is hard to give up the affinity felt in their nearness. Then, when the foliage is off and your sight-line longer, their size and great age are most striking, the spectacular, masked among the ordinary, made apparent.

Spectacular has nothing to do with scale. Once, I sat under those oaks in early fall, when a faint rustle in the fallen leaves was all that kept me from dozing in the warmth of the slanting sun. Most woods noises in fall leaves betray rapid bursts of movement—a chipmunk's darting, a squirrel's leap and scurry. This was different, a barely perceptible inching, a hushed lurch, announced by some single dried leaf coiling against another, so faint I could have mistaken it for an aberrant circulatory rumble inside my own ear. Yet, that determined rustling grew nearer, mere feet away.

Finally, I saw a leaf move, barely, and a dark mound, fist-size, lurched into view at my outstretched feet. Then, a shining eye, set in a docile head, rose to survey the ground, and a yellow-mottled shell settled itself for the next step. A box turtle, making its slow way forward, the soft rustling's stolid author.

I reached out and picked it up. It felt heavy for its size, as box turtles do. This was one of the rare box turtles that do not withdraw inside their sealable shell when handled. Its red eye glared from its beaked and scaled head, its bright orange legs flailed a deliberate turtle-flail, and clawed toes scratched across my skin.

The domed carapace was handsome with yellow, rune-like markings on a brownish-green background, each rune pattern enclosed in a geometrically distinct scute, and each of those ridged by faint concentric growth rings. I turned the turtle over to examine the plastron—its underside—and the head strained to right itself to continue its reptilian glare.

My fingertips played across the plastron's dark surface, which seemed to absorb light within itself, outwardly translucent over an opaque and featureless black. Once I'd stroked the plastron, I could not stop doing so for the sheer tactile mystery of it. It was the smoothest surface I have ever felt, so smooth there seemed no palpable boundary to it. With fingers resting on it, I could have believed I had not yet touched it. There was no sensory report of contact, only a disorienting sense of something outside my experience, beyond its possibilities. My fingertips caressed a surface polished against the cellulose of a million leaves, dragged across the buffing of algae and moss for days and nights within these woods. In its startling smoothness, a box turtle's underbelly is as spectacular as the Grand Tetons' jagged silhouette.

Spectacular can be as much about ecological context as it can be held in hand. Often, I've sat among those big trees and admired fox squirrels, a creature that appears entirely different in different regions. Geneticists believe fox squirrels are still trying to work out their evolutionary response to the changed eastern forests that followed the last ice age. One species everywhere, fox squirrels are black across much of the South, and silvery-gray along the Atlantic coast. In Appalachia, fox squirrels are a warm rusty-orange, blending to sulfur yellow on the belly. Their tail here is orange, with a ragged black border. Think "fall foliage" in fur; that's an Appalachian fox squirrel.

Fox squirrels everywhere, no matter their color, are also big—the biggest tree squirrels in North America. They can weigh nearly twice as much as the more familiar gray squirrel. They're also more sedate in behavior than gray squirrels; they seem never to hurry. They'll sit motionless in one spot, evidently entranced, for long stints.

When I hear an unhurried scratching on bark high in the oaks, I know a fox squirrel is near, maybe descending to forage on the ground. The ensuing moments will often reveal to me, brought up a squirrel hunter on the Greene County hills, the spectacular in the form of an arboreal rodent—one whose presence tells a story of context, process, and time. If the squirrel hunches downward toward me, then pauses, legs and tail outstretched against a sunlit limb, head up and alert in the sun, as if it were reveling in the pleasure of autumn rays, which it well might be, I am myself entranced in a spectacular presence.

Fox squirrels are less abundant here than when my grandfather took me to hunt squirrels under those oaks. But that's less tragedy than it is simple consequence. Fox squirrels prefer a different kind of woodland than grays. While gray squirrels favor extensive forest, fox squirrels thrive best in scattered woodlots and along woodland edges—the kind of habitats that dominated the hills when sheep- and cattle-grazing were at their peak.

I have read, and this excites me as one of the most spectacular concepts I've encountered about this region, that before European settlement, fox squirrels lived along the ever-shifting eco-border between wet eastern forest and dry western prairie. During wet cycles, forest probed west toward the Mississippi and beyond. In dry times, forest retreated eastward, back toward the mountains, and grassland claimed the vacated ground. For thousands of years along that capricious border, bison had trodden and grazed a blurred mix of woodland and grass. Fox squirrels thrived there, their numbers following the big oaks and hickories eastward or westward along the wavering grassland-woodland interface. There's a sense of spectacular in knowing that the patchy jumble of woodlot and pasture that cloaked Greene County's hills, where I shot fox squirrels as a boy for the family pot, where Angus and white-faced Herefords grazed in their placid mimic of bison, was a vestige of that prehistoric landscape. That feels no less spectacular than the migrations of whales.

The widespread reversion of abandoned rangeland to forest since 1960 favored gray squirrel expansion while it reduced habitat for fox squirrels. Since that's a natural consequence of forest reclamation, the fox squirrel's decline is less of a sting. But another factor in the decline, the explosion of invasive plants here within my lifetime, is dreadful. Fox squirrels prefer an open understory—park-like is one way their ideal woods are described—where they can forage on the ground and watch for predators. Today, any-place within these young, reverting woods where sunlight can reach the soil is invaded by multi-flora rose, barberry, and garlic mustard—thorned, snarling, or astoundingly prolific exotic plants that got a foothold within the last 40 years and now can't be stopped. Their tangled thickets clot the hills under the trees, too dense for fox squirrels. To call this phenomenon "dreadful" is a human judgment, far from the catholic lens advanced here. In that light, the rapid adaptation to and dominance of Appalachian wood-lands by invasives like multi-flora rose, and garlic mustard is a biological achievement of spectacular scale. Still, I yearn for the more native woods I knew in my youth, whose plants were less rank, distributed over the land not by a penchant for utter dominion but by some unseen protocol of shared space and light, known only among their various kinds.

That yearning demonstrates what a great debt we owe those prescient conservationists of the late 19th century who worked to preserve the Grand Canyon, Yellowstone, the Great Smokies, and so many other landscapes where native process still reigns, where it can be acknowledged and under-stood for the rightness it represents. We need those places in our increasing-ly artificial world for all manner of reasons. Despite my questioning here of their "spectacular" reputations and my direction of attention elsewhere, I do not wish to diminish their importance. Their importance is beyond words' ability to dim. But those preserved landscape fragments cannot ac-commodate all of us, and I've never found satisfaction in the idea that we benefit from wild conserved places "just by knowing they are there." I need contact. I seek immersion. Since I cannot travel to icons of landscape or of ecology every day, and because those hallowed places can't serve all our needs for contact, for immersion, without sacrificing themselves, there is also importance in cultivating an eye for the spectacular that carries on all around us. I first sensed that universal "spectacular" in the, some would say, unremarkable hills of Greene County. That was, I am sure, an accident of circumstance. Places much like Greene County, Pennsylvania, rim the Appalachian margins. All hold the spectacular within themselves, different from Denali or Yosemite only in scale. Up close, spectacular is wherever you find it, wherever it finds you.

Dunbar Creek;
Perceptions and Place

Here, streams shape life as in few places in America. To go anywhere here, streams must be crossed, which we now do without thinking, and streams flood, which we do not forget. Here, if you live in a quiet spot, you can hear a stream, conscious of it or not, ambient to your life. You absorb its timbre; your brain knows its tone. Even our way of speaking about an event that happened near a particular stream is telling. We tend to say the incident happened "on" Ten Mile Creek or "on" Laurel Run, as if someone walked atop the liquid surface, suggesting an intimacy with streams that is regionally unique. Because streams so clearly carved our topography, intimacy extends here to the slopes above a stream—its hollow on the local scale, its basin on a broader one.

You can sense intimacy in the way streams here got named. For some, think "branching tree." The North Fork of the South Branch of the Enlow Fork of Wheeling Creek tells you someone was paying attention when they came here. It tells you those who stayed knew to what their lives were connected. What's left of native language heired other streams their current names, as did people of more recent historical note. Creeks so named carry a hint of the past, like how a stream carries along that tint of mineral scent you can taste as you approach it in early spring after a winter sniffing sterile wind.

But intimacy does not mean our streams here were, or are, revered. Flowing water buoyed technological advances, but streams were obliged no deference, more likely to become sewers than remain pristine. Some streams absorbed even more fouling as if their abuse were a set upon mission instead of coincidental to progress, insults piled on in excess to subdue an uncivilized place. I grew up within the basin of a creek so beset. And when I began to think about such things, I wondered if my native stream had been sentenced to that fate early on, indicted by its own name—Dunbar Creek.

We lived in Fayette County, in Pennsylvania's southwest corner, on a modest knob called Rosy Hill at the western flank of Chestnut Ridge, the Alleghenies' western limit. Gist Run gathered itself from a farm-pond spillway trickle on the Ainsley farm downslope to the west where, as kids, we dammed it with mud, then breached our work to thrill to the brown torrent churning downstream, risking a chase by farmer Ted; and from a larger branch that sidled around Rosy Hill to the east. Neighbor kids and I crossed that eastern branch in the late 1950s on our daily walk through sheep pasture and woods to Mt. Braddock School, on a bridge my father built by felling two wild cherries over the flow, digging the lopped and butt ends into the banks, then nailing on boards and a rail. These two "cricks" joined to form Gist Run at Mt. Braddock, then flowed north to Dunbar Creek at Dunbar Borough. Some miles farther down and north, Dunbar Creek enters the Youghiogheny River at Connellsville.

Dunbar Creek was named for Thomas Dunbar, a colonel in British General Edward Braddock's 1755 campaign against the French at Fort Duquesne, built at the confluence of the Allegheny and Monongahela rivers, the site of present-day Pittsburgh.

Gist Run is another namesake of these events. Christopher Gist, the first white settler west of the Alleghenies, built a homestead on what would become Gist Run somewhere near where my father built our wild cherry footbridge to school. Knowing the terrain, Gist guided Virginia Governor Dinwiddie's envoy, George Washington, beyond the mountains in 1753 to warn French garrisons to vacate English claims. Washington was rebuffed.

Braddock made his final push northwest over the ridges from Wills Creek, now Cumberland, Maryland. To speed the advance, he divided his army, leading a "flying force" of 1,200 British regular troops and Virginia militia rapidly off the heights into the Monongahela Valley and assigned

Colonel Dunbar to hang back and command the slow trudge of artillery, wagons, and more than half Braddock's original strength. But when Dunbar reached the crest of Chestnut Ridge, he met the terrified, bloodied survivors of Braddock's rout by a smaller force of French and their Indian allies, streaming back from the carnage. Mortally wounded, Braddock died during the retreat and was buried in the crude road.

I think about Dunbar and Braddock when I top Chestnut Ridge, most often by car, on a clear fall day, and see Pittsburgh's crisp, urban skyline on the northwest horizon. They could not have known, by sight, the precise location of their fateful destination, as I can now. They would have beheld an unmarked ocean of random hills, wherein somewhere lie the Forks of the Ohio River, flowing west to the continental interior.

Dunbar had men and equipment for a counterattack, which might have changed the campaign's outcome. Instead, he burned all the supplies and joined Braddock's decimated remnant in retreat. Braddock's disaster, and Dunbar's flight, left the English frontier's scattering of settlers exposed to years of lethal raids by Indians hoping to hold onto their hunting lands and homes. Resentment over that vulnerability lingered until it diffused in the hum of the Industrial Revolution more than a hundred years later.

Every resource that served industrial awakening could be found in and gleaned from Dunbar Creek's basin. Timber was first to go and the most wholly exhausted. Workable, durable American chestnut climaxed the primal forest, lending its name to Chestnut Ridge, from which the creek springs. Chestnut and oak wood framed factories and mills, and hemlock bark streamed into tanneries. The rest of the timber went into charcoal mounds to feed iron furnaces, an acre of woods per furnace per day, and later into coal mines as posts. For decades, any tree, regardless of species, that grew to a size that could prop up a mine shaft was cut and hauled underground. Once cloaked by forest, sandstone boulders stood out on shorn slopes like grounded arks.

Narrow-gauge railroads probed up the hollows to carry in laborers and haul out timber, stone, clay, iron, and coal. Along the creek's lower reaches, railcars dumped their loads of refuse slag from the furnaces onto the floodplain, sealing the earth under an ossified gray shell that, in places, still caps the soil. When coke replaced charcoal as the fuel of choice in iron and steel-making, the already fevered extraction of coal erupted. The vaunted Pittsburgh bituminous seam, the world's highest-quality metallurgical coal, was nine feet thick under a third of western Pennsylvania, a thousand feet deep and out of reach. But along the northeast-southwest tangent at the western foot of Chestnut ridge, centered where Dunbar Creek emerges from the mountains, its subterranean pitch thrusts the Pittsburgh seam to the surface, where the mining technology of the day—human muscle and mule—could labor in a honeycomb of shallow but gas-seething, post-propped shafts to drill, blast, pick, and shovel it into mine wagons.

Most of the coal from the Pittsburgh seam went into coke, the remains of coal baked in long straight rows of "beehive" ovens made from fireproof brick. By 1920, forty-thousand coke ovens lit the Fayette County night lurid orange, blotting the noon sun in smoke. Most of those ovens lined the Youghiogheny valley and lower Dunbar basin.

Slate looks something like coal but is not, and young boys learned to know the difference. They picked through the coal as it came out of the shafts and heaped the worthless slate onto spoil piles around the mines. Coal dust in the piles caught fire to smolder and glow dully by night so that even during my adolescence, snow never laid on the reeking mounds. Nothing I have seen since resembles so precisely those scorched "red dog" mountains as photographs from the surface of Mars. Decades before, my parents forbade me to play near the dumps because "you'll break through and fall in"—to the inferno's core—Fayette County was at the nexus of natural resources and voracious appetite for them at Pittsburgh mills. Dunbar Creek's basin was the heart of that nexus. So, despite my naïve musings, and in fairness to Colonel Dunbar, the basin's subjugation had nothing to do with avenging Indian raids. It all would have happened that way even had Dunbar rallied, attacked the French, and emerged victorious at the Forks of the Ohio.

Males in my family had worked at the nexus as coal miners, coke rakers, firebrick kiln tenders and part-time hill farmers and were glad for it. But by the mid-1960s, when boys no longer picked slate at the mine mouth or carried water buckets to the coke oven tenders, my early acceptance into their society came mostly through hunting and fishing, though I did help my grandfather with butchering, haying and the last of the cattle. My first sorties to fish and hunt with these men struck me as profound. Most were flinty, sometimes grim, men whose ingrained concern was whatever work needed, or could be, done at any moment. Heavy work was supreme creed to my forebears, but when they took me to the woods for deer, grouse, or trout, they were like boys, an easy bliss on their weathered faces. I sense now that their release in the woods was my nod to explore, think about, and share what remained of the basin's natural character.

By the time I was old enough to roam the hollows alone, with fly rod or shotgun, a visitor who didn't know what to look for might never notice the vestiges of industrial boom in the basin, especially in the wilder Dunbar headwaters where the ruin had been less complete.

Demand for mine posts withered, so, except for chestnut, the woods had grown back so that you could walk all day and never emerge from the trees. Charcoal mounds were still there if you knew how to see them, covered by saplings and ferns, their contours worn. The old rail lines that followed the creeks were blurred by leaf-fall and frost heave, veiled in hemlock overhang, so they seemed placed there as footpaths instead of rights-of-way for steam-belching engines. A high adventure then was to ride those traces bareback on mangy ponies, imagining myself a western explorer. Even the iron furnaces, placed deep in the woods near the last of the charcoal sources, had slumbered to sulking stacks of expertly cut stone, lending oddly square ledges to sun-basking copperheads.

Gist, the run we lived on, is a peripheral, peopled tributary that enters Dunbar Creek well downstream. But the headwaters rise from a remote bowl girded by ledges that soar over jumbled talus. Mountain laurel traces the cliffs above rich woods, where trees of northern and southern pedigree mix. Beech, birch, and maple cling from that colder age when the face of glaciers loomed a hundred miles north. Magnolias, yellow poplar, and sweet buckeye pioneered from the south in the wake of Pleistocene thaw to thrive in sheltered hollows. White, red, or rock oaks, likewise southern, are everywhere, spread by seed-caching jays.

Brook trout were my prized quarry, then as now, and if you have held a wild brook trout across your wet palm in the fall, when it displays its spawning dress, fiery orange belly under slick olive back, speckled across all that in robin egg blue, you know at least one of my reasons for that objective. Yet, I remember being drawn to the contrast between the trees' stalwart permanence and the delicacy of wildflowers so that in spring, I often broke down my trout rod to comb the slopes. The bloom was initially hidden, trailing arbutus and hepatica, low and shy on southern exposures. I'd sometimes lay prone on the canted ground and press my nostrils down among dry leaves against an arbutus bloom, sniffing for its clear sweetness. When I'd indulge in such a thing, I thought of my grandfathers, laboring in dank darkness or searing heat, with some embarrassment, sensing it was a pleasure they could not have allowed themselves.

Days later gushed the exuberance of bloodroot, trout lily, Dutchman's breeches, and bellwort, then trillium that blanched ravine and streambank white. Enthralled, I marveled at the absence of crowds, come there to behold it all.

That marvel foretold an encounter. I was fishing with intent, a far hike upstream from the end of the road. The chattering creek muted other sound, so I didn't notice the intent troop approaching from behind me. Startled by a near voice, I turned to see two-dozen people dressed differently than the rare person I encountered back there. Their clothing looked new, even crisp, and seemed purposed, neutral-green or khaki. Some, men and women, gripped walking staffs, but they all looked fit, wearing newish good boots. Their ages ranged, but all were older than me. None were missing limbs, a common lacking among older men of my experience. Binoculars swung from necks, or a magnifying glass dangled by a tether. Most carried a small book or some journal stuffed in a pocket.

They were loosely fanned out along the streambank and cast their eyes over the ground ahead of their steps, the way my grandfather did when he took me into the woods for morels. Those people were interested in something, to the point of consulting guidebooks and sharing observations, but they carried not a sack among them. Whatever they sought bore no immediate utility to be cut, dug, or collected. This, like their clothes, set them apart.

They were friendly and curious about my fishing, so we talked. I learned they were embarked on the annual spring outing of the American Violet Society. They had assembled from across the country to explore the slopes along Dunbar Creek because, as their leader told me, its headwaters held one of the most diverse suites of native violets in North America. Like the trees, various wild violets had either migrated there or clung on as holdouts for thousands of years.

Learning such a thing about one's home ground, one's native creek basin, from a stranger from far away is a jar. In the way that my dad's and my uncles' missing work to take me grouse hunting gave me permission to enjoy the woods, the American Violet Society's acclaim for the basin's flora framed it as an exceptional place. Their pilgrimage pushed the slate dump smolder into its historical perspective, so I have since that day reveled in the Dunbar Creek basin's ecological resilience.

The ecology of any one place is complex beyond easy appraisal. Yet, some of the basin's living elements stand out to me as icons, a word to avoid because of its glib overuse, but it fits the purpose here.

Not everywhere, but at some scattered outcrops, if you climb up from the creek into cool shadows of boulders big as houses, you will be standing at the northern limit of the range of the green salamander, *Aneides aeneus*. This obscure amphibian hunts slugs and beetles in moist sandstone crevices across a range centered on the southern Appalachians, hub of the Earth's greatest radiation of salamander species. Green salamanders' bodies are compressed top-to-bottom and flattened to fit tight spaces. They shelter within boulders and cliffs from north Alabama, across eastern Tennessee, and along West Virginia's high spine. But they occur nowhere on Earth north of the Dunbar Creek basin in Fayette County, Pennsylvania. Here, at this one point along the 39th Parallel, they stake their extreme reach, where their need for cool, moist rock voids is last met, some individuals living out their lives within 40 feet of the crevice where they hatched. I wonder how they survived the logging boom and the mine-post shearing when sun must have baked their grottos. But this 3-inch creature's survival here proves the intact roots of natural integrity. Some semblance of best outcome is still possible here.

Wood warblers present the same testimony. Waves of them—more than two-dozen species—enliven the canopy every spring. Some pass on northward to fan out across vast Canadian spruce to breed. All spread widely to winter across the Gulf Coast or in tropical jungle after their southward fall journey. But here, because they need forest, they are confined to a narrow corridor along the Chestnut and Laurel ridges, whose woods funnel their flight as an hourglass tapers the passage of sand.

Many, the black-throated blue, magnolia, and blackburnian warblers among them, end their migration here to nest. Small birds, yet so significant by their presence, the warblers are not easily known. This seems a tragedy but a just one. Effort, here, yields great reward. Foliage obscures them, and they seldom hold still. Yet, to the resolute observer, they present such an array of colors, such varied patterns, that, shown pictures, the unfamiliar would assign them to some exotic place—Australia or a Pacific archipelago, to be known only from televised nature documentaries. To see these birds as they are, in early May, I have often climbed atop the same boulders that harbor green salamanders. From there, I could watch the warblers forage through the canopy at eye-level with the light upon them rather than silhouetted against the sky from below, which renders their plumage featureless black and anonymous.

I am not adept at knowing birds by song. But when I climb the boulders to gape at warblers, I can teach myself to recognize their calls by watching and hearing, at least for a year, when I must re-learn. If I watch a male black-throated blue posturing along a branch, then stop to thrust out his breast in wheezy, buzzing song, I will recognize that song later that spring when I'm fishing for trout. I'll know a black-throated blue is somewhere nearby in the hemlocks, even if I never see him, which is as satisfying as the tug of a fish.

Except for wild brook trout, nothing symbolizes for me the basin's wildness, its contrast to towns, like the timber rattlesnake. They're still there on some of the ledges. Somehow, they survived the logging, the fires, blasting their dens with dynamite, and two-hundred years of shooting on sight to wind in and out of the laurel shade as it suits them, almost impossible to see when sun-and-shadow fall across their rough, chevroned hide. They are protected now by legal constraint of the state, which means nothing to some. Still, if they made it this far, it seems likely some will remain, unaware that they represent for me both the native rightness of a place and my own evolving enlightenment.

I once shot a rattlesnake. I cannot explain why except that, at that time, we never thought of reacting to a rattlesnake in any other way.

We had been riding ponies across the mountain when .22 shots and yells drew our attention. I dismounted and walked toward the shooting among heaped rockpiles of an old quarry. A school chum and his father were probing around in the rock slabs, picking off rattlers with head shots where they found them coiled. They shot a half-dozen while I watched and dragged the limp carcasses out into the sun with long sticks. How can something be so visually striking—velvety black slashed across sulfur yellow—when dragged out of context onto featureless rock, yet be so hard to see when coiled, alive under dappled shade?

Later I returned with two friends and our .22s. We could find no rattlers in the quarry but happened onto an undisturbed outcrop, capped by laurel and huckleberry, in the woods nearby. When I stepped out of sassafras shade onto a flat rock shelf, a rattlesnake sunning beneath the slab uncoiled in a dash for shelter. Its head was already safe under the rock, so I aimed and shot it mid-body, which showed no effect except that the snake began to rattle, a dry, chitinous buzz that sounds like nothing else. The muffled buzz continued under the rock for a long time, and it claimed my remorse.

I never knowingly harmed another rattlesnake, though I now understand that what I did for a time had the same effect as a rifle. My closest friend, Curt, and I hunted and caught many rattlers alive. I know this had something to do with a drive to be among, part of, the wildest essence of the Dunbar Creek basin. You had to go to those kinds of places to find rattlesnakes, ledges tucked into rough terrain, blazing hot if you stood in the sun, reached only by long uphill hikes that nobody else attempted.

We displayed our captives in a cage out front of Rippling Waters, a kind of café and grill that was rustic before places tried to be, beverage service "unofficial," built around the walls of a defunct stone-crusher on the banks of Dunbar Creek. Tourists headed for the mountains by the "back way"—somehow before GPS—gawked at the rattlers coiled behind the screen before venturing inside or onto the back porch overlooking the creek to take a seat among trout fishermen, snake hunters, ginseng pickers, and pipeliners up from the flat country of Texas and Oklahoma, fearless in their straddling D9 'dozers to strap natural gas transmission lines over the steepest slopes they'd ever worked. Visitors got a delight on weekends when sturdy, aged men from the surrounding hills played fiddle, banjo, and guitar in their understated "old-time" style.

Although I knew most performers, could claim kinship to some, I craved their deeper acceptance. I played no instrument, so what felt like my way into fraternity was to supply rattlesnakes for the cage, which likely evoked amusement more than admiration. Since then, I learned that if you take a timber rattlesnake from its natal range and fail to return it to the same spot within a short time, the snake is doomed. Malnourishment is common in captivity, and a snake released in the wrong place won't find its way back to its winter hibernacula before cold weather. We did release our rattlers but didn't understand the importance of placing them back in the precise spot of capture. Females take eight years to reach sexual maturity, and gestating a born-alive litter is so taxing that they must bask in the sun for hours and weeks to stoke their metabolism, making them vulnerable to predation—and human capture. Those facts suggest that most of the snakes we took in our ignorance were gravid females, and our impact on the local population was severe. Today, I return to the rattlesnake ledges infrequently and only with a camera.

After so many references to brook trout, it may be a surprise that, ichthyologically speaking, the brook trout that still inhabited the Dunbar basin when I began to fish there were, technically speaking, not trout, but char of the genus *Salvelinus*. There are deeper differences, but most evident to the human eye is that trout—like the rainbow and brown trout (genus *Salmo*)—carry dark spots over a lighter background. Chars exhibit the opposite, showing lighter markings over a dark field. Pale-yellow, wormlike squiggles cover a brook trout's dark- or olive-green back. Char are northern fish of the circumpolar Arctic. The brook trout's nearest kin is the Arctic char, a fish of treeless tundra, fished by Eskimos, its sea-run populations pursued by seals slid from ice-floe lairs. To the south, somewhere this side of the Canadian tree-line, the chars blend into brook trout. They are native to the Dunbar Creek basin because the elevation along the Appalachian chain keeps streams cold enough to support them here near the southern limit of their North American range. The brook trout, then, represents a geographic opposite to the green salamander. Both are reaching their extremes here, pushing the envelope of tolerance, the salamander from the near south and the trout/char from the far north. But nothing about the evolution of char in the Arctic prepared them for Appalachian coal mining.

If you were to look at the color-keyed map prepared by the Eastern Brook Trout Joint Venture (various fisheries agencies and conservation organizations of the eastern states) to show the status of wild brook trout populations in subdivided watersheds across its native range in the United States, you would see mostly red, indicating "Greatly reduced." The brook trout's American range (excluding where it has been introduced, presenting an invasive threat to native trout in the Rocky Mountains) covers New England, upland watersheds of the Great Lakes, and most of New York state. Southward, the range funnels across Pennsylvania, broad in the north, tapering to a narrow band along the mountains in the southwest, the same taper the warblers follow in spring and fall. It continues to narrow across West Virginia and into the southern Appalachians. Red dominates that whole reach, with vast swaths of murky grey— "Extirpated"—around the margins.

A scatter of green ("Intact") flecks the map across northcentral Pennsylvania, headwater sources of the Allegheny River and the Susquehanna's West Branch, and the last best stronghold for the brook trout in northern Appalachia. Dunbar Creek's basin is red, except for titillating smears of yellow, meaning "Reduced," a slightly preferable status to "Greatly reduced." Brook trout are present but not what could be expected in an undisturbed watershed. My father and uncles told me the same thing in the mid-1960s that the Eastern Brook Trout Joint Venture map attempts to communicate now. Among the many tributaries that gather into Dunbar, only two held wild brook trout. These were Dunbar Creek's main stem itself, far upstream where my patriarchs called it "Little Dunbar," and Limestone Run, whose name suggests it benefits, from a trout's perspective, from some geological parenting unusual here.

By volume, the most important tributary in the basin is Glade Run, contributing half of Dunbar Creek's flow. It meets Little Dunbar at a fork that embraces what remains of the Center Iron Furnace, built in the "point" at the two tribs' confluence. In a geographic sense, it represents the "east branch" of Dunbar, descending through the basin's remote heart, mostly within what is now State Game Land No. 51. My father and uncles were not given to overt aesthetics, but they pronounced it a "God damned shame," that such a "beautiful" stream as Glade Run could not be fished. Their undisguised dismay was one of the strongest signals I had ever intercepted from my mentoring kin.

Every time I make the effort now to reach Glade Run, I remember their lament. It takes a considerable hike either way you do it, upstream along Dunbar's main stem or down off the top. Even without trout, it is a place that merits, and rewards, the effort. For one thing, wetlands are rare here, and Glade Run is born in one. It flows out of a winding flat, a glade, a large one for this region, part swamp and part marsh, where jutting snags and beaver dams convey a wild northern feel. Wood ducks and wood frogs are at home there. Oak-clad knobs rise above the glade on all sides.

Once Glade Run plunges off its plateau, you would never guess where it got its name. It alternately plumes, silvery-white, over the smoothed lips of boulders and rests in dark-green pools that absorb and exude the solemnity of hemlock shroud. Rounding any bend presents some new version of the elements of Allegheny Mountain trout stream—frothy cascade, smooth green run, stolid boulder, leaning hemlock, each juxtaposed in a different, yet perfect, arrangement. The friction between flowing water and atmosphere drags a cool current of air down off the mountain with it so that your cheek feels the caress, like the breath of a small child held close. In one stretch, the stream has etched its own bed downward through a broad and strikingly horizontal sandstone plane so that it forms what you can only think of as a "slot canyon," snaking through the stone in a constrained channel 15 feet deep and four feet across. During low flows, you can walk the stream inside an enclosed winding passage, a narrow band of canopy-screened sky overhead and fingertips roughing over grainy cool stone as you go. In a high flow, you would be churned to meaty slurry. No other place, in my knowledge, is like it.

Yet, despite its idyllic visage, when I began to fish with my father and uncles, there were no trout in Glade. Their "damned shame" was affirmed in the mid-1990s when faculty and graduate students from California University of Pennsylvania's Environmental Studies program surveyed the stream, finding no brook trout and scant aquatic insects that could support them. What bugs showed up in the Cal U. seines were those that could tolerate acidic conditions.

Brook trout are the most discriminating of salmonids. They require cold water, the kind that wells up from mountain innards. Glade Run has that, but it must be clean— "clean" being a term that takes in a lot. The chemical properties must be right, there can be no overloads of sediment or nutrient, and there's a fragile balance of acid and base that can't be tipped.

That balance in the Dunbar basin, in fact, in most streams across western Pennsylvania, tips easily toward acid. Our region's common geology lacks limestone, which, when it's present, blesses streams ushering from it with a property called alkalinity, the "buffered" ability to resist acidification from an external source, like acid rain or a coal mine discharge.

When I was born in 1952, the initial coal boom in the Dunbar basin was already over. But around that time, bigger and better equipment made surface- or strip-mining feasible to extract lesser (than the Pittsburgh seam) seams whose sedimentary position and the pitch of their uplift made them accessible on the mountaintops without sending men into shafts. Those coal seams cropped out on three sides—north, south, and west—of one of the knobs above Glade Run's wetland birthplace.

The long-abandoned 1950s strip-mine scars are still up there, across whole slopes, right down to the alder and cattail margins of Glade Run's natal swamp. You'd recognize the spot anywhere in Appalachia, yellow clay, scraggly alien pine trees stuck in the ground in pale attempts at reclamation, and crude, stony terraces to channel runoff. Sulfuric acid, the predictable brew that forms all across our coal regions when latent underground sulfur contacts the air, coincidental to coal's extraction, seeps or gushes out of the ground in dozens of places. When that acid first hit Glade Run, which lacked buffering limestone, it tipped the balance beyond the brook trout's tolerance. My fishing guides knew that, and when we hiked upstream with our trout rods and reached the forks at Center Furnace, they paused, gazed briefly up Glade Run, clucked their tongues, then turned right to lead me up untainted Little Dunbar.

There was no way, in their time, that my father and uncles could have imagined that anything could be done to remedy Glade Run's malady. Their only available reaction was to lament what might have been. Even now, that default still infects attitudes, so most people aware of the devastation of acid mine drainage assume stream restoration is too great a challenge. But something like living on one, fishing can endear you to a stream for life, and Dunbar Creek was "fishable" below the Glade Run confluence because Little Dunbar diluted the acid enough to allow the state Fish Commission to stocked trout there every spring. The principal worth of those hatchery fish was that they survived long enough to hook anglers on the place, some to imagine better possibilities.

I know people who came to care for Dunbar Creek in that way. In 1995, some of them founded the Chestnut Ridge Chapter of Trout Unlimited, an affiliate of the national organization committed to conserving and restoring coldwater fisheries.

Chestnut Ridge TU members all shared the view of my ancestors that Glade Run was too alluring a mountain stream, too otherwise perfect, to be without trout. But they refused to accept that absence as something they could not change.

They learned how to sample stream water with protocoled credibility, then hiked throughout the drainage, gathering samples. They raised money, gave their time, and won grants. They sought technical help from the Western Pennsylvania Conservancy's watershed office and waded into the complexity of getting regulatory permits to begin work.

In 1998 they began experimental "dosing" of Glade Run's main stem and two tributaries, Big Piney Run and Little Piney Run, with high-calcium limestone "sand," which is not truly sand but the finest particles of limestone left on the sizing screens at stone quarries after the stone is crushed for construction uses. The sand is so fine that it mostly dissolves in the water, unleashing the acid-balancing properties the stream's bedrock origins lack.

The dosing improved Glade's pH and alkalinity. Encouraged, the group placed hatchery brook trout in a cage in the stream. The trout lived, boosting their resolve and justifying more funds.

In 2003 they built a $300,000 anoxic limestone drain treatment system that captures and neutralizes much of the mine discharge into Glade Run. Soon after, teaming with California University of Pennsylvania fisheries biologists, they collected wild brook trout by electro-shocking Little Dunbar Creek, where a population remained, carried the small fish over the divide in watertight backpacks, and released them into Glade Run.

Within two years, Cal. U. biologists documented natural reproduction and two year-classes of brook trout fingerlings. Brook trout had returned to a secluded creek where they had thrived for 10,000 years, 3,000 miles south of their evolutionary roots, rendered once and briefly inhospitable by the single-minded exposure of coal beds.

Even after they built the treatment system, the group combed the mined-over slopes looking for more untreated discharges. They found many, so continued the limestone dosing in the Glade Run headwaters for nearly two decades. Their progress attracted more attention from the Western Pennsylvania Conservancy, whose more robust funding network enabled the WPC to build a larger treatment system on the old mine footprint, capturing "hot" discharges that bypassed the first facility. The water's chemical balance improved even more, though some leaching pollution remains to be captured.

In a regulatory initiative unimaginable to the men who took me trout fishing as a boy, the Pennsylvania Department of Environmental Protection proposed in 2018 that the Dunbar Creek basin, including Glade Run and its tributaries, 50 total stream-miles, be designated "Exceptional Value." An Exceptional Value classification places so-designated streams under the state's most vigilant shield of environmental protections. The proposal must run a tortuous bureaucratic and political gauntlet, the outcome unknown, but the Exceptional Value proposal, itself, proves an immense achievement.

A well-traveled trout angler who can fish where they want in the world—Montana, Argentina, Alaska—would consider Dunbar Creek's main stem still an under-achieving trout fishery. But it's improving, which is significant around here. More people value the stream now and take pride in it. I remember my father pulling his Chevy into one of the shallow fords across Dunbar Creek, clear water up to the hubcaps because it was acceptable then and natural to do. We'd all then pitch into the novel fun of washing our car in the creek, next to big-fendered Dodges and Plymouths whose owners were doing the same thing, our collective sheen of suds, solvents, and wax gliding toward the next downstream riffle. People don't do that anymore, maybe for lots of reasons, but among those is a consensus that treating a stream in that way is coarse.

Consensus about public spaces is never universal, and as proposed earlier, contact with a stream does not necessarily engender reverence. Some people still ride their ATVs along and through the streams, even on the state game lands where the rules forbid motorized play, strewing beer cans and eroding the banks, burying trout lily in an unctuous gray ooze. Such boorishness is fringe, though, as shown by Trout Unlimited's cleanups along Dunbar Creek on the Saturday before the opening of trout season every April. The group's commitment extends beyond the water's chemical health to include each visiting angler's aesthetic experience. Through all the years I've fished Dunbar Creek, a dirt road has followed it upstream to a dead-end well below the Glade Run confluence. It's known as Betty Knox Road, named for a spectral heroine of local legend. Betty Knox still walks that road some nights, it says, calling for her lost lover, a wounded deserter from the Civil War. The road is access for anglers, but it's also the kind of remote dumping-ground some people seek out. Even that pox has improved. The cleanups there once took an entire day and filled three PennDot triaxles with tires, bottles, cans, and castoff commodes. Now it takes a pickup truck and two hours to make the creek's accessible sections presentable.

For me, the people who worked toward restoring Glade Run and Dunbar Creek downstream represent a climax to a continuum. It begins with my father, uncles, and some of their friends taking me trout fishing on the still-healthy streams of the Dunbar basin, noting in their understated sadness the spoiling of the most attractive creek of all. Their dismay is illuminated by my recall of the American Violet Society field trip I met long ago while fishing. The violet-trippers knew about something still there in the basin; not just a wildflower but the natural resilience of a place left to its own, even for a short time, in this temperate part of the world. But that resilience did not extend to streams, which lacked the blessing of a limestone birth to temper acidification. Streams needed help to rebound, help that continues. The brook trout's absence from Glade Run diminished the lives of all of us who went there, even those who did not, because it was an absence from water, and within water flows our link to all ground above, our life's signature carried below.

Postscript

A recent conversation in which I took part hints that for people in some places, perhaps even here, contact with, indeed, any knowledge of, flowing water is fading. I share a summary here:

I was helping my aged mother write checks to pay her bills. She had lost the pre-addressed return envelope for one bill and was anxious about what to do. A phone number on the statement invited a call with questions.

"I'll just call this number, tell them you lost the envelope and ask for the address," I assured her.

A courteous young woman answered my call. When I explained our dilemma, she provided the accounts-payable address in Carol Stream, Illinois.

She spoke rapidly, and the town's name was unusual and unfamiliar, so I sought confirmation.

"Is that Carol, like a woman's name?" I asked.

"Yes, Carol, just like a woman's name."

"And is that second word stream, like a small river?" I pressed.

There was silence on the line, then, tentatively, "No," and she spelled it for me. "It's S-T-R-E-A-M, stream, like when you stream a video."

Then I fell silent.

When I'd recovered enough to thank the young woman for her help, I hung up and related the exchange to my mother, who is 93. She is understandably challenged by some abstractions now, but she grasped the significance of the phone receptionist's focus. My mother has never fished in her life, but she knew we kids dammed the outflow from Ainsley's pond because she had fielded Ted's complaints when the breached impoundments chewed at his pasture. She was there when her husband built a bridge across a fork of Gist Run, from wild cherry trees that grew on its banks, to get us kids from "the hill" to school. She had washed many wet, muddy clothes and knew I could not sleep on the nights before the men took me trout fishing.

She will likely be gone soon, and with her, that small piece she held of our collective knowledge of streams as flowing water. The Dunbar Creek basin conferred to her that part of her life. She absorbed it unsought from a current never ceased.

Culture in Tomatoes

I have read that modern humans are made more susceptible to infections and ailments by a diet that is too sterile, too effectively disinfected. Hyper-processing of our food, at least in developed and industrialized parts of the world, makes natural elements and organisms that humans have long ingested coincidentally with food unavailable to us. So, our immune systems become impaired.

That idea always returns when I stand in late summer in the afternoon sun of my garden, to eat a ripe tomato out of my hand, as one would eat a drier and less-luscious apple.

Just plucked, the tomato is warm and firm but yielding, with a heft that seems too great for its volume. As my lips grate against the fine veil of dust that lies across the smooth skin, my breath flaps a shard of spider web that flags from the stem, my eye spies a spatter of white bird chalk on a leaf where the fruit had hung and I feel smugly fortified against the creeping anemia of an urbanized food chain.

Just before I bite down, I smell the resinous oil, rubbed off a leaf by my fingers and hinting of an incongruous, yet appetizing, blend of mint and kerosene. The tomato's turgid skin resists, relents, then gives way, gushing tart juice across my chin and through my fingers, flooding in with viscous seeds I can never clamp between the points of my teeth. Devouring the whole fruit takes a combination of biting, slurping, sucking and lapping maneuvers that reduce it to a yellow cone of flesh pointing out from the base of the stem. My teeth and mouth feel cleansed; my fingers are sensitized but not sticky.

Tasting, smelling, and feeling all of this, the sun on my skin is a palpable weight. Among the tomato plants, the sunlight seems to accumulate, to build up and exert its force with more power than elsewhere, as if the vines had evolved the ability to hold it there, milking it slowly, defying the Second Law of Thermodynamics, which states that, except in a tomato patch, nothing—not plant, nor machine, nor man, can convert all the energy it receives as light, fuel, or food into useful work.

Tomatoes are as enigmatic as they are luscious. Descendants of a wild South American nightshade, sensuous and vulnerable, here they grow with abandon in a sometimes gritty region. Long before I had thought about them in the context of nutrition or impoverished immunity, they had been a way to ground myself in a place and to trace a thread of custom and community already on the wane. In simplest terms, tomatoes have been a temporary annual triumph over cold gray winters. But here, prized and pampered tomatoes were a way for people to excel within the limits of a time and place that, for many, held few options.

Where I grew up, the first ripe tomato of summer was an object of high status. Men would start the seeds in hotbeds in late winter. You could see the beds placed haphazardly around out-buildings, along lanes, near heaps of machinery, or beside the garden but always accessible to early spring sun. All these hotbeds were improvised in some way, never "store-bought" or ordered from catalogs. Old doorframes or railroad ties arranged in a rectangle, then covered with glass, were common components. It was not unusual for the glass covers to get crashed by a neighbor kid's baseball, the weight of a wandering dog, or even the boots of the owner who'd forgotten its whereabouts under the season's first snow.

As the spring progressed, men would gamble against the frost to set out their plants as early as they dared. Some who went about the same unvaried routines in their work, sleep, and church would experiment with tomatoes, striving for fruit that would ripen before their neighbors and co-workers. Some planted their vines in rotten cow manure heaped inside worn-out tires to hold the heat. Others lined the garden with sheets of black plastic or planted along the southern walls of garages, sheds, privies, or coops that would absorb the sun and exude warmth.

The spreading vines of early summer always ignited the controversy: to stake or not to stake. Staking, that theory held, yielded fewer fruits, but those produced would have fewer flaws. Plants that "ran wild" through the garden, said the advocates of that method, sprouted more tomatoes but the blemishes the fruit acquired from lying in the damp shade would not hurt you anyway. Those with enough room hedged their bets and grew tomatoes both ways; on sprawling vines for the loads of fruit their wives would transform into spaghetti sauce, juice, and catsup, and on stakes for the perfect pomes to be shown off and given away to less-skilled gardeners.

Prized as a tomato stake was the roof bolt, a 6-foot, ribbed steel rod with a silver dollar-size steel disc welded to one end. Roof bolts were driven into the overhead roof of a coal mine to hold up the ceiling of the pit section being actively worked. But according to some who used them for both purposes, the bolts made better tomato stakes than roof anchors, and they found their way out of the mines by the thousands. Vines entwined neatly up and around the bolts, and the red globes of fruit hung down in the sun so that a well-kept garden suggested a rank of spears hung with shields and armor during a lull in some Roman conquest.

Sometime around mid-July, amid resting knots of miners, mill workers, carpenters, loggers, or road laborers, one of the men, without a word all morning as to what he'd planned, would proudly pull that first ripe tomato from his dinner bucket to eat there in front of the others.

Alternative bites of tomato and sandwich—likely chipped ham, baloney, or bacon on homemade white bread—he would glance around the dinner-break (dinner was the noon meal) circle to be sure that everyone had noticed his prize, while the juice cut canals down his forearm through the morning's accumulated grime.

"I got lots of green ones bigger'n 'at," someone would say, posing as unimpressed. "Mine'll be ready next week."

Another controversy would return with the foggy mornings of mid-September. Some people believed they could prolong the tomato season by wrapping green ones in newspaper and stacking the paper-wrapped fruit in cardboard boxes for storage in a dark cellar. They claimed they could go downstairs at Christmas and retrieve a ripe red tomato. Others maintained that the newspaper method was a sure way to produce an inky, smelly mess in the cellar, and since there was no way to improve on the vine-ripe tomatoes of summer, they accepted the end of the season and ate the green ones as pickles or fried. Piquant and hard, sliced and breaded in crumbs or flour, then browned in hot lard, fried green tomatoes made the last garden suppers of summer.

In all the countless conversations I have been a part of about tomatoes here in my home region, I have never heard anyone pronounce the word "Toe-may-toe," as it is spelled or as you might hear it read aloud. Always the word comes out a bit abbreviated, altered, or slurred. I've noticed "T'may-duhs" or "T-may-tuhs" or even "D'-may-duhs" with a more insistent beginning. The older mountain people I knew as a boy said "maters" as if they wanted to get to the heart of the word with no pretension. In all these dialects, the hard "may" of the middle syllable is always there, but attention to the syllables on either side of "may" is casual and optional. I have always felt that these wayward pronunciations revealed a familiarity with and fondness for the fruit that you will not hear from people who buy their tomatoes at a grocery or who have never staked a bit of their own identity on growing the first red tomato of summer or canning a coveted quart of sauce.

You don't see roof bolt tomato stakes as much anymore, or hotbeds or laborers eating summer tomatoes like apples. Likely as not today, they bought their lunch at a Quick-Stop store on the way to work. You rarely even see gardens now between the bigger, newer houses or set amid wider, neater lawns. Of course, prime tomatoes are still prized by everyone everywhere, and they fetch a fine price at truck farmers' roadside stands. But the time it would take to work a patch of ground, transplant the seedlings, tend the plants, then preserve or even gather the fruit feels like something beyond our reach, like a dream related from someone else's sleep that we can't imagine being real for ourselves. A tomato is a small thing in the scope of our world, but what can you share with a neighbor when you've finished mowing the lawn where there could have been a garden?

Surviving Summit Mountain

Snowbound residents of Pittsburgh's hilly neighborhoods may not share this view, but part of the appeal of being a Western Pennsylvanian is that our natural geography still imposes influence on daily life. Not all regions enjoy or endure that dash of topographic spice, but it's inescapable on my travels over and atop Summit Mountain, looming eastward above Uniontown in Fayette County.

As you ascend the Summit on Route 40, glances at your car's thermometer will affirm that it's reliably six to eight degrees cooler at the top than in town. Even an older vehicle and your own body will register the change. The windshield will fog halfway up, and your ears will "pop" in response to dwindling atmospheric pressure. Those degrees ticked away on the climb are a summer delight, but the temperature range is often greater in winter. Snow can fall on the crest when rain is dimpling puddles on Uniontown streets. And once snow falls up there, it crusts and lingers, a tier of white soaring above sere lowlands, hinting of more dramatic topography in alpine places.

Truckers and parents of school-age youngsters pay the closest attention to the Summit's weather. Trailer rigs caught in a mountain squall paw to a standstill just short of the crest, blocking the way for more winter-nimble units, or slide and jackknife on the descent. "I hope I can get back over the mountain before it snows" is a common seasonal mantra among residents of Chalk Hill and Farmington who work in Uniontown. Snow days in the Uniontown Area School District are a "tail-wags-the-dog" affair, governed by conditions on the Summit, even though the three mountain townships that make up 80 percent of the district's land area account for just 26 percent of its population.

Some of the mountain's moods are less benign than a two-hour school delay. Planes have crashed in the fog that envelops the skyline knobs. The murky fog can brew in winter or summer, and when it obscures the Summit, it's not unheard of to encounter drivers who lost their orientation on the crest, then headed down in the up-bound lane, on the wrong side of the barrier, their lights emerging from the vapor ahead at the last avoidable moment.

Even clear skies merit caution. Route 40 boasts two lanes heading east and two lanes heading west on the mountain's flanks. But both the east-bound and westbound lanes taper to one lane each way at the top, bottle-necking traffic over the crest. Aggressive drivers don't like the slowdown, but it saves lives. Within those tapers, at the Summit's crown, Route 40 traffic comes up suddenly on opposing intersections, one heading north and one south, where the steep grade renders sight-distance nil. Building passing lanes across the top would be deadly.

Through the 1960s, a broad sign stood at the Summit on Route 40's westbound berm: "WARNING: 3 PEOPLE KILLED BY RUNAWAY TRUCKS SINCE 1960." At some point, the Pennsylvania Department of Highways (now PennDot) crossed out the "3" with an X and placed an adjacent "4" on the same panel. The sign is long-gone, and the runaway truck ramp halfway down has largely stemmed the threat. But when ascending from the east, overhead signs still warn of the imminent westward plunge: "DANGEROUS MOUNTAIN AHEAD," lending adventure to routine commutes.

If you have never crossed the Summit, don't imagine it as a stand-alone peak. It is a summit only in the context that it's where Route 40 (The National Road) scales Chestnut Ridge. At the westernmost flank of the Allegheny Mountains, the ridge slants northeast-to-southwest from a point east of Indiana, Pennsylvania, to about Grafton, West Virginia, where it peters out into plateau. Our contemporary ridge is what remains of the western ramparts of a much higher Appalachian system heaved upward when continental land masses collided 300 million years ago.

Today's heavily wooded ridge is 2,000-2,800 feet above sea level and 1,200-1,500 feet above the rumpled basin to its west. Where Route 40 tops Chestnut Ridge, the Summit stands 2,418 feet above the seas. The only gaps in its 100-mile span are at Blairsville, Latrobe, Connellsville, and Morgantown, where the Conemaugh River, Loyalhanna Creek, Youghlogheny, and Cheat rivers, respectively, cleave the ridge. Looking west along the Summit's latitude, no more mountains rise until Colorado.

One of the best places to view Chestnut Ridge is from the parking lot of Uniontown's Target store. Nearly the entire breadth of the ridge, south to north, spreads out before your eyes. It's an amazing geographic spectacle in a region attuned to more intimate views among wooded hills, and you wonder why the city of Uniontown has never capitalized on this prominent feature in its branding. We sometimes fail to "see" our natural landscapes, lulled to complacence by their dependable presence.

And there is much to see on the ridge at different times of the day and year. In early morning, with the sun rising behind it, the ridge presents as a dark wall, a featureless monolith. That carries its own allure as stark division between settled terrain and wilder reaches, reinforced for me by mountain encounters with rattlesnakes and bears.

In the evening, especially in winter when the sun arcs farther south, the light strikes low and oblique along the ridge's flank, incarnating its relief across that entire expanse—ravines and hollows, folds and off-shot fingers, outcrops and crags. Then, you can sense the subtle but relentless work of weathering across an unfathomable gulf of time.

When oak leaves still cling, November sunsets are lovely, melancholic, and fleeting. From the moment you first notice a plum tint, through deepening climax, to the quiet bleed into umber, you'll heave only a handful of breaths. But these are awestruck breaths, snatched while wondering what blend of tangential ray, aspect, bark, rock, and weathered leaf can strike the eye with purple light.

More enduring than November purple is the pale green of spring, with its chance to witness deciduous renewal climb the mountain's face. Green appears first in the sheltered hollows. From there, it oozes upward, tentative at the advancing fringe. Once the green creeps out of the coves, it vaults up the open slopes, racing toward the crest until, weeks after its birth below, new green erupts atop the ridgeline. Sometimes, during this progression, a spring snowfall caps the green advance with a white mantle across the crest. If afternoon sun accents the contrast, the visual impact can lure traffic on far-below and parallel Route 43 to the shoulder.

Change reverses direction in autumn. A coppery tint flares first at the top, then flows downward as it kaleidoscopes to scarlet, yellow, and orange. There are always outliers, though, scattered trees that enflame at random, outside the advance, obedient to some internal code.

Seasonal transition presents a primer in woodland ecology—why various trees occupy the places they do. Those bright-greens of spring, and the butter-yellows of autumn, showing in the same sheltered hollows, are the foliage of tulip poplar (not a true botanical poplar, but a magnolia). Poplar needs the deeper, richer soil that collects in coves. Dark-green blotches tucked into those coves are hemlock, which clusters along streams that drain the slopes. Hemlock doesn't show seasonal change but stands out in winter when hardwoods are bare. Leathery swaths along the spine and across the sidehills indicate oaks, which favor drier soils. "Benches" and terraces anchor smears of burnished coppery-gold, the persistent leaves of American beech. Beech holds its wizened foliage long toward winter and does best on "flats" where the soil is deeper but not too moist. Most rare, and impossible to detect in summer, are the wispy, gray-green bands of Virginia pine and pitch pine. These pines cling to the poorest, driest, most exposed and wind-battered ledges shunned by other trees. Seen up close, rooted to their outcrops, pines here convey a sense of desolate wildness, less familiar than bucolic woodlots below.

A dark irony is that the one tree missing is the one that gave the ridge its name—the American chestnut. Our native chestnut was extravagantly abundant throughout Appalachia, useful and fruitful when the region was settled. Western Pennsylvania was the heart of its range. But American chestnut succumbed to an invasive fungal blight, imported on Asian chestnut transplants. Beginning around 1900, every chestnut from Alabama to New England died within three decades. Several oak species have assumed the niche chestnut filled in our uplands, but the chestnut blight is widely considered the most tragic ecological calamity ever to befall North America.

Poignant lore recalls the chestnut's dominance on the ridge. From early childhood, I remember the sadness in the voices of my normally stoic elders, telling of shoveling up wagonloads of chestnut burrs crammed with sweet, nutritious nuts as the blight drew near. Long before that, settlers plodding west over the Alleghenies on a trail that became The National Road and then Route 40 thought they saw snow atop the last, westernmost crest in June. Days later, when they'd reached those heights, they gaped under a vast canopy of American chestnut's white-catkin flowers.

The antagonists never noted them in their journals, but the chestnuts were there when this summit hosted bloody history that shaped today's politics and national boundaries. Just north of where Route 40 crowns Chestnut Ridge, British colonial officer George Washington and his native guide Half King skirmished in May 1754 with a small, surprised party of French and Canadians led by Ensign Coulon de Jumonville. Accounts of the clash conflict depending on which side wrote them, but Jumonville's grisly death there sparked the French and Indian War by which England, after a series of defeats, won control of the contested Forks of the Ohio and colonial dominance in America. One year later, British General Edward Braddock's army marched west and north over the same high ground on its way to disaster on the Monongahela, where Braddock, Pennsylvania stands today.

Except for the absence of one great tree and away from roads, the ridgetop appears much as it must have to Washington and Jumonville. Sandstone boulders dominate, some big as houses, with girths of jumbled talus around their base. Overhung thickets of rhododendron and mountain laurel soften their ruggedness for the eye but not the foot. The timber seen from below strives upward among the rocks.

Most notable, if you venture far enough from the roar and hum of Route 40's corridor, is the quiet. Normally, we are immersed in noise, and as we move away from noise, its ambiance clings. So, the quiet is not obvious when it first assumes primacy. But, at some moment, quiet will enfold your attention, "louder" in its own way than accustomed clamor. Atop the ridge, your ears are above all noise except the wind. The wind is not noise; it is sound and so belongs.

On a clear day on the ridgetop, especially in autumn, you can see Downtown Pittsburgh between gaps in the timber. Its crisp silhouette on the northwestern horizon juts from an ocean of wandering hills, settling into prairie and plain.

The Ecology of Old Barns

Forty summers have waned away since this barn held the bustle, the laughter, and the 400 bales of hay put up by a family at work together. Forty summers with no flecks of hayseed stuck to sweat on sun-tanned forearms, and forty winters without the warm, sweet scent of cow breath in the feedlot underneath, the heifers' and steers' snorted exhalations rising above the frozen clods and the pies of steaming manure.

The barn was old even then, its beams and buttresses hewn out by hand before the Civil War. The barn stands deep in a Greene County hollow, shadowed by hills where turkeys and deer thrive in woods that reclaimed the pastures of what was once foothill sheep country. Now, the barn stands as the last bastion against irrepressible forest.

Study the barn from afar and the inevitable, if valiant, surrender is clear. The barn is a magnet and storehouse for heat—the sun's energy, especially on a day in late winter. Its dark bulk intercepts the slanting rays and stores them, leaking them later as gentle warmth. The barn's southern and southwestern corners ooze out warmth the dark timbers absorbed in daylight, setting up a milder micro-climate where the long-gone farmer's wife's daffodils sprout earlier than anywhere else on the farm. Fat green spears of pokeweed jut through here while snow still clings in the hollows, and blackberry canes blush red before the geese fly by headed north.

Wild grape claws up the corner and over the roofline. Near the roof's peak, the grape vines knit together with the branches of a massive sugar maple that stands in the barnyard, just as they do in the nearby woods, foreshadowing the structure's imminent fate. Each fall, cedar waxwings perch and flutter among the tendrils, picking off shriveled wild raisins in the afternoon sun.

On the shaded and cooler eastern and northern walls, poison ivy crawls and clasps, twining around the window vents and embracing the hinges. Bird nests hang in the tangles, and the golden twists of parasitic dodder climb and grope among the ivy. Together, they veil the northeast corner in shaggy gold.

The grape, ivy and dodder hold the moisture and block the sun, tempting fungus and mold to suck slowly on the fibers of wood. Gradually, inexorably, their weakening dampness and the weight of their own tissues will pull the walls to the ground.

Inside, it takes a moment for the eyes to adjust to the dim. Everything inside is dominated by the beams, thick and stout as engines. They soar throughout the superstructure. On their flat sides are the etchings of an adze, hieroglyphs in a sylvan temple, left long ago by someone who accepted long hours of hard work as the nature of life and knew how to convert his skill and a raw resource into the components of an agrarian world.

On the sides of some beams are scraps of bark bearing an unfamiliar pattern. It is, one older mentor once said, the bark of American chestnut, never seen in its maturity by two whole generations of American people. Chestnut once dominated these hills, carpeting the woods with a bounty of nuts that neither man nor beast has ever known the equal. The native chestnut, useful and durable, was not good enough for all early Americans. Some planted the Asian chestnut import, with its choking fungal blight, and the only American chestnut bark to be found over half a continent now is hidden in the haylofts of barns that slouch in hidden hollows.

In an interior corner, the end of one massive beam is exposed. A flashlight cast across the grain to enliven the texture pulls 175 growth rings out of the shadows within the squared geometry hewn from the original log. There is no way to know how many of the most recent rings are gone. Still, assigning this beam an age of only 175 years at the time of its felling to build a barn standing since the Civil War, the tree would have sprouted sometime around 1690. Even at the conservative estimate of 175, this tree, long-now a beam in this barn, was birthed at about the same time as

William Penn's land grant colony, far to the east on the Delaware River. This beam stood somewhere on these hills before their location was ever surveyed and recorded, before the concept of land ownership ever surfaced west of the mountains. Wolves must have howled beneath its branches, and panthers lolled along its limbs. This wood is a silent brooding link to a place and time we can scarcely imagine.

The interior north wall, below ground level, is a masterpiece of simple stonework. The stones are lain, one to another, as if the builder were guided by a formula for placing numbered pre-cast pieces instead of a random yield of native stone. Nowhere are there voids or bulges; the seams run straight, and the wall stands true.

The wall offers yet another testimony to a probing sun. All along the wall, the bottom courses of stone are covered by powdery green moss. About two feet above the earthen floor is a sharp line of contrast—green moss below, the cobweb-crusted, gray stone above. The green must mark the part of the wall accessible to the late evening sun just before it slips beneath the ridges. Never, in the 160-odd years since the wall's erection, has the sun kissed the upper courses, and no green shows there. Similarly, there are no cobwebs on the green stones, where the sun licks daily for a fleeting few minutes. Only in perpetual shade, apparently, do these arachnids ambush and stalk.

A neighbor still summers a few Herefords here, and they most mark the feedlot below the loft. Their steps have hooved the soggy ground into rounded mounds, and their hairs are caught in the splinters. Kick one of the mounds, and the searing rush of ammonia drills up your nostrils and probes at your brain. Your eyes smolder. Wait until they clear, then look closer. Other signs come clear, tracks of raccoon and opossum, mouse, and rat network the withered puddles of bovine urine.

On the flat sides of some of the beams hang the mud-and-hay cupped nests of barn swallows. The mud must come from the floor, churned to mire by the summering cattle. The grasses and shoots of hay lie parallel, spiraling around the nest like the arms of a galaxy but cemented firmly in the mud. Swallow nests are fewer here than in the past, owing to the slow encroachment of forest on the open pastures the birds require for their aerial insect hunts. Only one sizable pasture remains, on the barn's north side, where the cattle trod and chew the pioneering woods. There, the remaining garrison of swallows swoops and wheels in the heat of high summer.

More abundant now and nearer to the doors and windows are the haphazard, loosely strewn nests of starlings. The starlings are more forgiving of their surroundings. As long as enough cattle are around in summer to drop piles of organic debris, the starlings will stay. But when the barn finally falls, when native woodland overwhelms its foundation, the opportunistic starlings will move in closer to town where the pickings are easy.

Plastered on the ceiling is the chalky yellow "nest" of the organ pipe mud dauber wasp. The female wasp gathered mud from the floor and carried it up to the ceiling in her mandibles. There, she would have shaped it into chambered tubes, each cell primed with a spider or insect paralyzed by her venom. She would have laid one egg on each mummified arthropod. When the young wasps hatched, they would have fed on the corpses entombed there with them, then clawed out of the tubes of mud into the light, temporarily sated.

Once, entwined about the feeder slats was the papery shed skin of a rat snake, silent patient hunter of dark, tight places. There is no skin here now, but there may be again. Then, it will be picked up and shredded by starlings and sparrows, then carried into the rafters or ivy to cradle eggs the snake itself may relish before the chicks ever appear to their parents.

At the base of one interior wooden wall is a bit of bone, a little bigger than a car key and the color of coffee with too much cream. There, in deep shadow, solar rays have never bleached it white, and it seems to have absorbed the darkness. It looks most like the pelvis of a groundhog, carried inside, perhaps, by a fox. Or maybe the chuck died beneath the piles of wood and tin, and mice scattered its bones.

In the loft, accessible from ground level on the north, on the few moldering bales are piles of scats—dark, dry, and spindly. Their shape and size suggest coyote in a spate of hard times. Packed tight together, with little hair to hint at affluence, are the chitinous brown wings of June bugs and some scraps of ant. It would seem that, at the time of the June bug, the woods and pasture should have been alive with young woodchucks, rabbits, and mice. And the warm swampy stream in the bottom would have throbbed with frogs. But who knows why the hunting was hard? Maybe it was just this one coyote that was hindered by injury or disease. Maybe that's why this coyote came into the barn and not the others, healthy and hunting bigger prey. Or, maybe coyotes just like the taste and texture of June bugs. The scats don't tell you much beyond the obvious.

The barn is not so much a system unto itself as it is a way station, a conduit and a respite. All manner of creatures seek shelter and food here for themselves and their offspring, then return to the forest and field. Pokeweed and dandelion exploit the place, for now, warmed by stored sun and shielded from competing plants by the trudging of cattle. They, too, will move on to other hospitable, if temporary, environs.

Lying alone on the rotting floorboards is one powdery-gray owl pellet about the size of a joint of your knuckles. Around it in the straw are a half-dozen feathers that could be from an owl. They are "fluffy," with lots of what a fly-tyer would call marabou at their base. The whole feather is cream-colored except for darker chevrons along the shaft. The bird books don't show enough detail, but the feathers speak "owl."

Inside the pellet are four or five elegant ribs, curved and graceful. They look like the leavings from a well-groomed woman's session of fingernail trimming. There is also a jaw, a third the width of a dime and scalloped to hold an anchor of muscle. The teeth are still chisel-sharp, stained dark as walnut husks. Their owner represents a dead-end in natural selection for its kind but life itself for the owl. This mouse did not fear the open darkness, did not sense death's silent strike from above.

Downstairs is something that beckons back for one more look. It stands on a whitewashed ledge under a veil of dust, dead insects, and cobwebs. It is a Mason jar, wide-mouthed, seal intact. Inside is some dark indiscernible substance. Beets? Applesauce? Beans? Whatever it is, it was not intended to wait here, cadaverous, in the silence of so many decades. The jar is a tiny metaphor for this barn itself, filled for the future by hopeful hands, holding within itself a link to the past in a chain that is long since severed.

Under Plovers' Wings

Some things come into and go out of your life before you grasp their worth. For me, as a youth, it was that way with the birds and the baling.

My family made hay on fields at the Alleghenies' western foot. The work was hot, long and dusty, and I chafed at the toil while pals swam in the river or loafed in town. But my father and grandfather were stern about work, and I was bound to it.

This all passed in the days before self-loading balers that flip the hay into random heaps. We walked loose and strong in the sun, flanking the wagon while the Farmall tractor chugged under my grandfather's tanned hands, heaving every "square" bale—higher with each tier—to an esteemed "stacker," some neighbor or kin who could knit the bales together, so they held as a swaying, lurching unit.

The birds lent to the work a dreamlike air. They still do when I recall it, maybe because I have never seen them again. They rose from the stubble and beat low flights ahead on slim, pointed wings, then swooped upward in the very act of settling back down. Alighting, they reached for the grass with long, trim legs and thrust their wings high, like feathered pennants, before collapsing them in a deliberate and elegant fold.

We did not know what they were and would not have learned if not for a friend. He was a big man and gruff but gracious, with the unlikely first name, Julius. A coal miner by job and a deputy game warden by choice, he knew about birds, and he knew they were upland plovers.

They nested in that field, he said, and nowhere else for counties around. My patriarchs were intrigued, but we had hay to make.

The plovers stayed for awhile, perching on posts to assess our intrusions, pealing out their strange yipping whinny, audible if you flushed them on foot or a bareback pony, away from the tractor's cough. How can you grant adequate weight to an encounter like that when you've known so little of a broader world? The plovers were strange to us, relict of western prairie, synchronized to long-gone bison hordes and January summers on Argentine plains. Their acceptance of substitute Herefords did not extend to hay rakes. Their hemispheric roving could not abide corn rows or sprawl. They are gone now from that place, even their name, which ornithologists changed to upland sandpiper.

And how can a sullen kid know how rare and proud it is to work in the open among family, pressed on by impending rain? I muse about having them both back to relish anew—the baling and the birds. Yet I know I was lucky to be there at all, in the hay-dust under plovers' wings, so long ago.

Highland Marvels

Desirable and Otherwise

Red Oak, White Oak

Were it all to happen at once, the earth might quake all the way to Pittsburgh's Point. From early September through late October, acorns fall from their parent oaks all across the Allegheny ridges. Healthy acorns can weigh as much as nine grams each—a pound or so to the 50-count. When oaks seed abundantly, as they do in loose cycles of several years, an acre of trees can push out a quarter-million nuts. Rough math and an assumption of average mass tell you that, in those autumns, two-and-a-half tons of starchy seeds rain down on every acre of oak woods soil.

It's been hard not to think about acorns lately. The nights have been warm, and the windows open. Through the night, they clatter and boom on my woodshed's aluminum roof. This fall, the acorns are abundant, heavy and dense. All kinds of things happen—and do not—when oaks drop heavy "crops." To the relief of landscapers and gardeners, deer disappear from gardens and lawns—drawn to oak stands back in the woods; trash-raiding black bears vanish from the edge of town, but corners of attics that red squirrels and mice can get into mound up with smooth brown nuts. Acorns, when abundant, dump a flood of carbohydrate into the food chain.

If you hunt for your meat or know someone who does, you can see, even feel, the metabolic payoff this plenty affords. One October morning, I killed a deer with an arrow on a bench of white oaks above the Youghiogheny River. It was an acorn-rich autumn, and I'd watched the deer feeding for a long time before I shot. It nuzzled through the leathery fallen leaves and lipped acorns into its mouth, then lifted its head to chew while the eyes scanned the woods. I could hear the strong cusps crushing and grinding even as fragments of acorn fell and pattered on the leaves beneath. Then the doe would scoop up another nut and repeat the chewing. So many acorns littered the ground that the deer did not need to step ahead to find more. It stood, anchored, and nuzzled, ground, and swallowed, time and again.

Later, after I'd hung the deer in my shed to cool, its hide pulled off with a clean crackly sound and left a waxy feel on my fingers. Under the hide, dense white fat encased the doe's sides and back, sheathed two inches thick across the saddle and hams. Even my skinning knife was slick with fat, bouncing the lantern light off its greasy blade.

That dense fat left the same fine oily feel on my fingertips as the inside of an acorn cut in half. The deer fat and the acorn had, in fact, held the same oil, had each been the same oil, in different forms for the respective objectives of an oak and a deer.

Even a squirrel reveals the value of periodic oak seed abundance to wild things. When acorns lie everywhere, squirrels carry paired pads of almond-colored fat, not unlike your thumbnails in size and shape, on the small of their back and a sheath of clean white suet astride each kidney.

More intriguing, though, than the extravagance oaks can display is a loose harmony that has evolved among the different oaks themselves and all the wild things that reap their bounty.

Our region has two recognized categories of oaks—white and red. White oaks, perhaps, are the more familiar group to the casual observer of arboreal detail. They are more often the oaks of campus and square, near but largely anonymous, spreading shade yet somehow obscure. Most white oaks, though, are "wild," rooted in broad flats at the flanks of ridges, studding narrow benches along the contours or re-colonizing abandoned fields. White oaks are most readily told by the lobes around the leaf margin. White oak leaf lobes, seven to 10 in number, are round, like the pendulant lower extremity of the human ear. The bark of these trees is whitish-gray, finely flaked and with shallow fissures.

Red oaks, generally more common, are better known to those who leave town to go into the woods. Hikers and hunters know the darker, "rangier" impression a red oak makes on the eye. Their bark suggests a tightness to the trunk, accented by long, narrow, plateaued scales. Red oak leaves bristle dagger-like spikes around their margins. Red oaks often command sites that are drier, stonier and steeper than white oak haunts, but the two are also likely to grow side by side.

Each group has worked out its own style of acorn-making, and each group's acorns their own way of sprouting new trees.

White oaks have, across 60 million years, found an advantage in getting right down to business. White oak acorns mature in one season. The same germ of tissue that erupts from clustered white oak flowers in May falls to earth that autumn as a complete seed.

Once on the ground, white oak acorns continue their sprint and germinate fast. Go into oak woods in an early October when white oaks fruit with abandon. Their brown acorns, stained yellow at the "shoulders," will be everywhere—piled against roots, strewn on the moss, puddled in leafy depressions. Thrusting from the apex of every one that's been on the ground for more than a few hours will be a fleshy white radical root, ready almost from impact to nose into some cleft and begin sucking water and sending out hairs.

Red oaks approach this business with less haste. Though each spring sees new red oak blossoms grace a particular tree, the resulting seeds take two seasons to mature. Every one that drops on your hat as an acorn this autumn appeared as a flower 18 months before.

Like their parent tree, red oak acorns are more contemplative after their fall. They drop at the same time as white oak seeds, but the ample globes lie there, waiting. After a wet, cold autumn lying among the leaves and after a winter under a ceiling of snow, red oak acorns sprout their first rootlet the following spring, two full years after their airy birth as an oak bloom.

Even as the oak seeds rain down, a subtle harmonic force exerts itself on the future, worked out through tens of millions of years of quiet experiment and adapting, of opportunity seized and of reproductive flops and successes. It is a fluid force that we don't think of in the context of forest and fauna. It is the pervasive force of selection, driven by acorn taste.

To sense what's at work, peel the tough brown skin off a red oak acorn. Bite the oily yellow meat inside and chew. Within the time it takes to draw a breath around that odd bolus, its bitterness will crawl all over your tongue. Even after you spit, which you will, shreds stuck between your teeth will leak their vile essence.

After the ability to analyze taste returns, do the same with a white oak acorn. The flavor is mildly bitter, almost bland. Chew long enough, though, on a big enough bite, and you will sense its mealy nutritiousness but get no pleasure for your trouble. At that point, suppress your own conditioned perception of "sweet," hyper-juiced as it is by processed syrups and industrially concentrated cane. If you can achieve that suppression, you may grasp the taste that, in nature, qualifies as "sweet" and tempts mice, wood rats, deer, squirrels and bears to walk across red oak acorns to gorge on the seeds of white oaks.

That bitter taste, more powerful in the red, is the sensory signature of tannin. All oaks, all plants, in fact, hold tannins in their leaves, stems and seeds. Oaks possess more tannins than most other plants, and acorns hold more than other oak tissues. We humans are no strangers to tannins; they impart the desired tang to coffee and tea and that edgy zest to walnuts. But don't think "coffee" here because its tannin is tame compared to an oak's. And in a can of mixed nuts, no acorns nestle against the pecans and almonds, each of which holds a bit of its own tannin. Acorn tannin is too bitter and too concentrated for human snacking.

Even an expensive wine's pleasantly bitter essence comes from tannin, in the skins of its own grapes and from consort with an oak barrel's innards.

Bouquet is one thing, but, in nature, tannins have real purpose. Their bitterness tells of their complex ability to ward off bacterial attack, inhibit fungal rot and discourage ingestion by animals. Plants developed tannins as protection. Too much tannin can even be toxic to a plant's attacker, blocking protein digestion and the absorption of essential iron. Thinking evolutionarily, then, if you are a plant that produces a large, conspicuous and calorie-packed seed to empower your own seedlings, that seed will need protection. Given enough time, ruthless competition, and the imperative of reproductive success, you might come up with bitter taste as its safeguard.

Not that that taste can't be overcome; it's just costly in money, work, or time. Native Americans in what is now California and Arizona didn't need the former but did lots of work when they made use of oaks' bitter windfall. They gathered acorns, stored them in baskets and soaked them in streams for months. The flowing water leached out the tannins, rendering the seeds bland but edible and nutritious, ready to be pounded into flour for bread or thickening for stews of deer meat or fish. Sadly, we know almost nothing about acorn culture among Native people who lived in the vast Allegheny oak forests. But surely they used acorns in the midst of such bounty.

Our own culture's most extensive involvement with tannins had nothing to do with taste or with oak. For two-thirds of a century, beginning before the Civil War, loggers felled the great hemlock forests across northern and western Pennsylvania for the tannin locked in hemlock bark. Great dark trees a hundred feet tall all across the mingled watersheds of the Allegheny and Monongahela rivers were cut and peeled of their bark, then left to rot on the naked ridges. Flatcars of bark trundled into tannery towns around the forest fringe, where it was cooked in vats, rendering a caustic liquor that could tan leather. All the harnesses that pulled America from an agricultural economy into the Industrial Revolution were cured with tannin leached from the bark of headwater hemlocks.

Acorn-eating among indigenous peoples probably arose in Eurasia, then spread east and north to where oaks couldn't grow. After humans crossed the temporary Bering Isthmus and filtered down the western spine of North America 20,000 or so years ago, they rekindled oak culture on the slopes of the Rockies, then spread it east, learning along the way what deer and wood rats already knew, that acorns of white oaks are "sweeter" than red. In handmade baskets sunken in streams, white oak acorns needed less time for leaching, and in the woods, yet today, in autumns when both kinds of seeds are there for scooping up, deer, squirrels and mice seek out the white oak seeds first, as a matter of taste.

But that presents white oak with a problem. Its relative sweetness dims its prospects for seed survival and reproductive success. To compensate for its appeal to seed-predators, white oak evolved the ability to germinate fast. White oak strives to send up seedlings before it's too late, before a deer grinds the seed to spittle and meal.

Meanwhile, red oak nuts play their waiting game of winter dormancy, rooting in the spring when their seedling can't freeze. But they hold more than bitter tannin inside their husks. Lying there bitter and spurned, red oak acorns reveal yet another tier in this elegant harmony among oaks and oak-eaters. Besides being less appealing, at least initially, red oak acorns are also more nutritious. They contain twice the protein, carbohydrate, and four times more fat than white oak seeds, even after months of soaking in rain and snow melt. So, as wild things nuzzle aside red oak acorns in early fall in favor of white, they unconsciously reserve the red's nutritional punch for early spring when little else is available, when they will need it the most, and when the bitter taste of red oak tannin has leached away.

To sense the fuller complexity of these adaptations, consider that taste and caloric content are not the only differences these trees have devised in their seeds. To fulfill their respective strategies, each tree had to work out an appropriate design for the reproductive packet it dropped beneath its limbs. Nowhere are those designs more apparent than in shape.

The white oak acorn is relatively slender. Mathematically, its ratio of surface area to volume is high, a design that allows water to infiltrate the seed's interior quickly, jump-starting germination. Conversely, the shape that most inhibits water infiltration by maximizing the ratio of volume to surface is a sphere, the geometry most nearly copied by a red oak acorn. The red oak acorn's globe shape allows it to survive continual soaking until conditions are right for sprouting in spring.

Shape may be the clue birds use to select among acorns, to the limited point they do. Grouse and turkeys stuff their crops with whole white oak acorns early in fall, possibly because they can cram more of them in. But, generally, studies indicate that birds don't distinguish between white and red oak acorns in the same way as mammals do by taste. Blue jays, for instance, are ravenous acorn foragers and consume red oak acorns as readily as white.

Scientists observing jays eating red oak acorns early in fall wondered what protected the birds from toxic concentrations of red oak tannin. Subsequent dietary experiments reveal that jays have no built-in protection from tannin poisoning, specifically to tannin's disruption of protein metabolism.

But this ballet goes on and on with an ever-wider cast. Acorn appeal extends to the insect realm as well, and anyone who has examined a dozen or so acorns will have seen the evidence. A tiny circular hole, about pin-head size, in the husk of an acorn that feels lighter than it should, testifies to the exit of an acorn weevil. That weevil's parent laid its eggs on the fruit at some point in acorn development; the larvae fattened on the flesh inside and then chewed their way out.

What seems to be at work is that in randomly consuming acorns, a jay coincidentally ingests just enough protein-rich weevil larvae, and enough of the weevils' own tannin antidote, to keep its own system well-fueled yet unaffected.

Oaks, of course, get something out of this interaction, too. Jays are seed hoarders. Besides the acorns they eat on the spot, they carry others to new locations far from the parent tree, where they stash the nuts in tree cavities or shallow soil. Oaks, then, offer up a conveniently carried and durable packet of food in exchange for a mobility they themselves can never know.

And it isn't only the jay that pays back the oak. Taking a long-term look at a forest unmasks the weevil's vindication. Long thought to be a threat to oak forests, weevils actually help oaks to spread by protecting the acorn-carrying blue jay from the oak's own tannin.

Our familiar way of thinking about forests holds the danger of delusion that one acorn's impact, among millions, is inconsequential. Nothing could be further from the honed truth of eons—that every cell and every process are parts of an intricate whole, born out of blind and urgent struggle, each participant seeking an edge in the broad palette of life in these woods where we live.

Dance of the Vole; An Allegheny Encounter

The snow was scant airy powder, two or three inches deep. I know this because I was skiing a bony trail through hardwoods and hemlock in the Allegheny Mountains toward where Meadow Run joins the brawling plunge of the Youghiogheny River. Gouges in those skis document that day when the urge to ski in a winter of little snow overwhelmed good sense. It had been cold, though. At dawn, the thermometer on my woodshed read -11°F, and by early afternoon, when I got on the trail, the air had warmed to 8°.

This trail descends the face of a ridge through laurel and rhododendron understory that softens the slope's harsh complexion of boulder and ledge. Entering a glade where the rhododendron thins, I saw, scribbled across the steep bank to my left, the track of a small animal on the snow. The maker's trail, wide as a thumb, gave an impression of panic inconsistent with that quiet place. The creature had looped back across its own trail, again and again, describing ovals eight inches long and half as wide. Not counting the ovals, the trail's general course was down-slope toward my own, and within a foot of where my skis creased the powder, the track went berserk. It coiled over itself in tight orbits no bigger than a baseball, then trampled densely over an area with the dimensions of a computer-mouse-pad. From the "pad," it made short probing peninsulas, at the limits of which the animal had reversed direction to return to the trampled pad. At the remote end of one probe lay a rich-brown sphere, much like a table-tennis ball, except it was cloaked in glossy pelt.

I stepped out of my skis and crouched closer. An equator of warm red encircled the sphere, and its "poles" heaved in and out. I scooped it up with shards of loose powder. It was weightless in my gloved palm. Held there, the furry ball revealed detail.

The hint of a head, short and tapering bluntly to a rounded snout, tucked tightly inward. Somehow, the head appeared bear-like, with two rounded ears mounded scarcely above the fur but was no bigger than a thimble. An arc of orange incisor showed at the muzzle, and two tiny, flat-black eyes anchored an otherwise featureless face.

Gently, I unfurled the furry globe, which became a chunky bar of body the length of my middle finger. Its back was lustrous brown with a rust-red stripe running from head to the base of a brief tail. Long black guard hairs lay over the dense fur. The sides were smoke gray, while the belly beamed warm, golden tan, like coffee with generous cream.

I pulled off a glove and found the pencil in my breast pocket. With its point, I lifted the whiskers from where they sprouted at the snout. The whiskers reached easily back beyond the ears, but there was no stiffness to them, no resistance. Lifting against them was like lifting the winter air. Had I not seen the glint of light they reflected, I would not have known their length from the feel. Gloveless now, my fingers stroked a pelt so fine, soft and void of warmth that I could scarcely tell I touched it. The creature made no attempt to resist, panting heavily in my palm. I formed it back into a ball and reached to place it back at the end of its last desperate probe. There, where I'd missed it initially, spread a half-dollar-size stain of urine on the snow and four black turds, smaller than rice grains cut in half. I positioned the creature atop its last leavings and resumed my ski. When I returned a couple of hours later, it was dead.

The animal I'd found was a red-backed vole *(Clethrionomys gapperi)*, secretive microtine of these mountains. These shy rodents don't offer up encounters on every walk in the woods. Despite my frequent rambles along these hardwood ridges, this was the second red-backed vole I had ever seen and, curiously, the second one I had held in my hand.

Years before, when my daughter Colleen was in junior high school, her science teacher assigned a project that, in some way, employed the "scientific method"—advance a theory then test it. At about the same time, the maturing oak, cherry and poplar timber on the tract adjoining our home was logged. That event, the first logging of those woods in 60 or 70 years—a long span in this region's forestry—seemed an apt subject for Colleen's investigation.

She accepted my offer to assist, so I borrowed several small "live-traps" (aluminum boxes with a bait pan and spring-tripped door) from the Wildlife and Fisheries Department at West Virginia University. In an admittedly crude wielding of the scientific method, we hypothesized that logging had reduced the diversity of small mammals living in our neighboring woods. We set three traps there, baited with peanut butter, and three others with the same bait on a similar east-facing but unlogged slope within Ohiopyle State Park.

To Colleen's delight, we caught things immediately. Amid the tops and slashings near home, we caught chipmunks and white-footed mice—lithe, leggy rodents whose prominent ears, tails, legs, and snouts all seemed to reach out to engage and grasp and whose big expressive eyes tempted affinity.

A few miles away, around the mossy rocks and roots in undisturbed forest, we caught the same white-footed mice and chipmunks, but we also found in our traps woodland jumping mice and one red-backed vole, whose stubby nature and tiny bead eyes made a clear morphological counterpoint to the elegant white-footed mice. Our experiment hadn't necessarily indicted typical Appalachian logging as a menace to biodiversity, but we did observe a difference in mammals caught, with identical methods, on the two types of sites. But something about the vole, perhaps the warm-red pelage or the cubbish head, skewed the project's scientific objectivity, for Colleen pronounced the vole "cute."

We decided to keep it temporarily in a terrarium at home, and Colleen named it Templeton.

The vole lived there for weeks under bark and moss, venturing out to eat nuts, to drink, or to test the tank's glass limits. After Colleen had submitted the assignment, her objective became showing Templeton to her grandmother, who would soon visit from Norfolk, Virginia. But on the afternoon she arrived, Colleen ushered her grandmother to the vole's confines, expecting scurried rustling beneath the moss. But there was none. Her vole had died that morning.

* * *

Red-backed voles live in diverse forested places across North America, Europe and Asia, the breadth of the northern hemisphere. In North America, their range forms a broad, swooping swath from southeast Alaska across boreal Canada to the Atlantic Coast. But a distinct and narrow peninsula of red-backed vole habitation juts southward along these hardwooded Appalachians as far as northern Georgia. That same continental range pattern, spread broadly and homogenously across the northland, then probing south along the cool Appalachian spine, is seen in other, more familiar, wild things. The brook trout exhibits it, as does the wood frog and ruffed grouse. Several wood warblers also sing widely across Canadian forests, but farther south, at American latitudes, only on these high, narrow and wooded heights of the Appalachians.

The mountains here are cool enough to harbor northern species, but those species all show adaptations to life at the limits of their range. Most Appalachian ruffed grouse are "red," while northern birds in Canada and around the Great Lakes are generally gray or "blue." Our mountain grouse are also adept at finding and digesting acorns, a calorie-dense morsel that mid-Canadian grouse, which thrive on aspen buds, would not recognize. Brook trout in the Appalachians are better equipped to live through droughts when their headwater creeks shrink to damp trickles.

The red-backed is one of roughly 70 vole species that scurry through the world's forests, deserts, tundra and grass. Just as Colleen did, taxonomists distinguish voles from their near relatives, the mice, by their low, rounded ears, shorter furred tail and short hind legs. Voles are compact creatures at home in tight runways, wriggling beneath snow, matted grass, in voids amid underground rock.

Season dictates red-backed diet, which is likely more diverse here than farther north. In spring, they eat grasses, stems, bulbs of herbaceous plants, and whatever leftover acorns, beechnuts, cherry pits, or other seeds they can find from the previous fall. Fungi, blackberries, blueberries, and other fruits enhance the summer fare, as does the occasional cricket or snail. Autumn is the season of seed-eating and, since voles are active all winter, they forage then through crevices and under snow for seeds, roots, dried grasses, bark and subterranean fungus known as endogone, that grows in close association with the roots of trees.

Voles, in turn, fuel much of the forest fauna. Timber rattlesnakes, black rat snakes, mink, foxes, and owls all hunt red-backed voles—snakes in summer, owls in winter, weasels and foxes throughout the year. Researchers in Nova Scotia noted the first recorded appearance of predatory long-tailed shrews on their study area, and a simultaneous but temporary crash in the numbers of red-backed voles, indicating that voles stoked the shrew expansion. In response to passing so much energy further up the food chain, red-backed voles are procreative athletes. Females bear as many as three litters during their lifespan of 10 to 12 months. Litters can be as large as eight young, born after an 18-day gestation. Sexually mature at 10 weeks, red-backed voles may live their whole brief life within the duff of a quarter-acre of forest. In favorable habitats on the Allegheny Mountains, more than 150 red-backed voles might live within 10 acres of woods. Despite my own rare encounters, they are thought to be the most abundant rodents in forests across their range.

Despite their terrestrial preference, red-backed voles are said to climb trees sometimes, but I have never seen one climbing. Dark-pelted, finger-length voles might climb with abandon and still escape sight. Some references also say the red-backed confronts mice and other intruders in its territory with a shrill chattering call. How do humans come to know such things? The chance of spying a tree-climbing red-back is far greater, I would imagine, than hearing that muffled cry. Would it emanate from beneath the snow, from under a root? Would I know what it was if I heard it?

How long, I wondered, had this vole I'd found while skiing been there, tormented in fresh powder? What had driven it across the snow to this end, and what explained its contorted course?

The snow had fallen the previous day, so any history scrawled upon it had occurred sometime since. The vole's looping trail to its death recorded what is known among mammalogists as "waltzing," a behavior of various small rodents, always in response to some disturbance or distress. A Guide to the Mammals of Pennsylvania describes waltzing as ". . . a condition in which the animal makes rapid, circling movements from left to right and jerks its head."

If some predator disturbed the vole, the snow held no sign of the attack. No fox had nosed and pranced in pursuit along its path. No weasel had burrowed and plowed. No owl had left prints of its primaries behind. The tracks' loops, probes, and retreats indicated some internal torture.

One possible culprit was the cold and snow, or, rather, the relative lack of snow. The temperature had plunged the previous night. This I knew even at my home on a hilltop. Who could know how much more frigid it may have been in the pre-dawn stillness in that secluded ravine? Against that cold, the scant snowpack offered little insulation; mere thin chaff that scarcely held my skis off the rocks. I pictured the vole in panicked, shivering flight, its metabolism struggling to generate more heat than it spent, instinctively seeking a ceiling of deep snow like those that had sheltered its ancestors through the Pleistocene freeze.

Snow is generally considered a challenge for wildlife, but it can also be an ally. Search the literature of snow as an ecological influence, and W. O. Pruitt, Jr's work of five decades will be the first to emerge and most persistent throughout. Born in Maryland and raised in Virginia, unlikely latitudes for his life-calling, Pruitt studied snow and how animals and plants are affected by it from Alaska to Newfoundland from the 1950s nearly until his death in 2009. His work demonstrated that snow, at least in northern regions, is not a uniform slab across the land. Rather, Pruitt learned, long-lasting snow is a diverse, ever-changing, evolving feature of landscape, as powerful in its influence on living things as soil itself.

Pruitt was not your typical academic. While working for the University of Alaska in the early 1960s, his opposition to Project Chariot, a plan to blast artificial harbors in the Alaskan coast with nuclear bombs, derailed the scheme but cost him his job, as well as the chance to do field work or teach at any university in the United States. Welcomed at Memorial University in Newfoundland and later at the University of Manitoba, Pruitt was equally at home in the lecture hall or a tent on the taiga, and he counseled his students to temper their classroom learning and, more recently, their "keyboard ecology" with authentic experience in nature.

It was Pruitt's insistence on using native Eskimo language to describe snow in all its moods and forms that impacted our understanding of snow as an ecological variable. "The English language evolved in a misty, maritime climate where snow was an uncommon occurrence," Pruitt wrote in a 2005 article in Canadian Field Naturalist. "Consequently, it is woefully deficient in words representing snow phenomena. The 'scientific' languages (Latin and Greek) are derived from cultures which had even less familiarity with snow and its various forms than did English."

In most of his nearly 100 scientific publications, Pruitt baffled orthodox academics but said what he meant and described what he saw with Kobuk Valley Eskimo words like *anniu* (an-nee-you), which describes falling snow. Among the Kobuk Eskimos, *api* (Ay-pee) is snow as it lies on the ground; *siquoq* (see-cok) is windblown snow; *qali* (kall-ee) is the snow on tree branches; *upsik* (oop-sik) describes a hard consolidated snowpack unmoved by wind or, in some contexts, blown snow deposited by wind in a hardened drift. Particularly important in Pruitt's observations were "*zaboi*," (za-boy), depressions in the tundra surface that accept and hold *upsik* for long months. Pruitt used this alien but perceptively articulate vocabulary to describe with keen precision conditions that both challenge and shelter snowbound mammals.

From the subnivean mammal perspective, one of snow's most important properties is what Pruitt and the Kobuk Eskimos call "*pukak*" (poo-kak). Pukak describes a base layer that can sometimes form under the *api* (snow lying on the ground). It happens only where snow lingers long, but the earth's surface emits enough modest heat to melt the snow immediately above, but where the air above remains cold. Liquid water, then, refreezes against snow higher in the column, creating open "channels" or voids in which small animals can move about between snowpack and soil.

On tundra, where Pruitt worked much of his life, he learned that *pukak* forms every winter, especially over *zaboi*, or tundra depressions. Arctic and sub-arctic small mammals seek *pukak* for shelter as long as it lasts. Thus, Pruitt showed some of the earth's regions assumed to have the harshest winters—which, in fact, they do in the air above the snowpack—actually provide some of the most stable environments for small mammal survival.

Pruitt's knack for seeing the whole ecological "picture" enabled him to demonstrate that snow can work both ways, even for an ice-age success like the red-backed vole. Pruitt's field studies of snowpack in Newfoundland moved him to challenge a long-held belief about the absence of red-backed voles from Newfoundland Island. Only the meadow vole is native there, where it lives on grassy fields and seashores that the winds can blow bare. Canadian biologists long held that red-backed voles did not inhabit New-foundland Island because the Gulf of St. Lawrence and the Strait of Belle Isle blocked range expansion from the mainland. But Pruitt argued that an island-wide lack of *pukak* and not a 10-mile-wide strait, prohibited red-backed colonization. Red-backeds would have gotten across the straits somehow, sometime, he reasoned, but could not last the first winter under wet island snow.

It snows heavily in Newfoundland, but moist, relatively warm wind bathes the island every winter. The result is that warmth flows down through *api* (snow on the ground) from the air as well as up from the earth, and *pukak*, with its channels and voids, never forms.

"I interpret the reason that there is but one species of vole in New-foundland is not the failure of other species to cross the Strait of Belle Isle, but the lack of a *pukak* layer," Pruitt wrote. "The animals would have to spend too much energy digging through the dense, heavy maritime snow cover to survive on this island."

There was, of course, no *pukak* in the woods above Meadow Run where I found my vole, and never has been, at least in the past 10,000 years. Snow is not something that elicits close inspection in this part of the world. It falls and melts in cycles of days. It's mostly considered a hindrance to driving on hilly, winding roads. Plowed industriously by crews from the township or state, it's gone from the roads with the next afternoon's sun. Only along the highest ridges does it linger long enough to constitute even a semi-perma-nent seasonal feature. So, Appalachian red-backed voles, living along the southern highland prong of their species' range, have apparently made do for millennia, in far milder winters than the Kobuk Valley, with whatever episodes of protective snow they got, and despite occasional storm events that mimic the warm wet snows of Newfoundland Island. I thought that maybe the previous night's conditions had posed a perfect meteorological "conspiracy" against small mammals—unusual cold for this region, but with no real snowpack for insulating protection.

Even here, snow can blunt a cold snap's edge down at a red-backed vole's level. A 1979–1981 study of red-backed vole winter metabolism at

Powdermill Nature Reserve on Laurel Mountain in Westmoreland County, Pennsylvania, found that voles fared well and even gained weight through those winters despite air temperatures as low as -18°F in January 1981. Even then, the subnivean microclimate, where voles foraged and rested, offered a comparatively steamy refuge that never dropped far below freezing. But unlike the thin powder in which I tracked the waltzing vole on Meadow Run, researchers recorded a snowpack a foot-and-a-half deep during the worst of the cold and at a consistent depth of eight inches for more than a month. Curiously, though, they noted no other snowpack properties in their report, as Pruitt would certainly have done—whether or not it had grown compacted by wind, been altered by daily cycles of freeze and thaw, or had stratified through successive snowfalls, all of which can influence a snowpack's innards. A graph they produced shows the air temperature rose once during that span to 44°F, presumably at mid-afternoon, but snow depth remained constant, suggesting more snowfall soon afterward, with layered tiers of varied density upon the ground. The snow through which my disturbed vole plowed, looped and probed had scarcely more substance than the air itself.

Still, if a night of arctic cold was the source of my vole's stress, and if an acre of these woods can harbor dozens more red-backeds, why did my skis cut only one waltzing trail? Why hadn't the cold routed out the whole population along my course? Why hadn't my "waltzer" simply sought deep recesses among boulders and rock, as had, evidently, all others of its kind across that slope? Maybe my vole had strayed into the musty, root-haired haunts of a territorial rival, which had banished it into the open with a shrill and chattering call.

If cold had not killed this vole, and if no tormenting predator started its flight, then what explained its waltz?

Scientists studying all manner of physiological phenomena have observed, even induced, waltzing in voles and other rodents. Mice and rats have been made to waltz in laboratory cages in response to excessive noise and light, and pathologists note waltzing as a symptom of infection, inflammation of the inner ear or neurological disorder. With some considerable effort, researchers investigating the transmissibility of chronic wasting disease (CWD) to rodents sharing the range of white-tailed deer caused captive red-backed voles to contract the disease. CWD is a deer-borne, brain-eroding disorder akin to "mad cow" that certainly "disturbs" its victims. Since red-backed voles are known to scavenge deer remains, and because CWD's infection-inducing prions remain viable for years, the researchers wondered in their conclusion if these rodents might be an inconspicuous reservoir of a disease that only becomes apparent when contracted by large mammals with which humans interact, such as white-tailed deer.

A review of the staggering, wandering, drooling symptoms shown by deer with advanced CWD makes it plausible that a vole with the disease might waltz, and CWD has been documented in deer in Hampshire County, West Virginia and Bedford County, Pennsylvania, both about 70 miles from where I met the waltzing vole above Meadow Run. But despite the researchers' experimental "success," there is no known CWD connection between deer and red-backed voles or any other rodent in the wild, and in no way in nature could voles be exposed to CWD prions in the way the researchers infected them in their lab—by intra-cerebral injection. Still, diseases are as adept at seizing evolutionary opportunities as are mammals or birds. If there is a survival advantage for CWD in jumping the deer-boundary, the disease will likely find it if it has not already done so.

What is becoming known is the role of red-backed voles in the health, spread and restoration of the very woodlands in which they live. It is a subtle but powerful role, carried out in quiet and dark, in each vole's own self-interest, to the subsequent and coincidental benefit of a planet.

Red-backed voles eat fungus to an extent that is only now being grasped by people who study such things. Not surprisingly, familiar fungi and fungi parts, like mushrooms, "toadstools," and morels, are part of their fare. Harder to note, voles in their wriggling and scurrying amid the crevices where tree roots have probed and pried, also eat the underground fruiting bodies of endogone, a broad genus of subterranean fungi that infect, in a "good" way, the root-hairs of trees that tower above. Microbiologists call these fungi "ectomycorrhizal" (living on the outer surface of plant root hairs) and have named about 5,000 species worldwide. They acknowledge, though, that this known slice likely represents only a fraction of the underground fungi that spread through the planet's soils.

In their symbiotic embrace of root hairs, these fungi, in exchange for the tree's spare carbohydrates, make it possible for roots to absorb water and nutrients from the soil in which they are anchored. Endogone not only partakes of this mutualistic union; it defends it. Somehow, it deters attacks on the tree by destructive pathogens, ensuring, in turn, its own inconspicuous future. Striding among sturdy boles as we do at the earth's airy surface, sliding our hands across textured bark and noting the dappled light, we tend to assume that a forest owes all to its sun-catching canopy. But the truth, we are learning, is that a forest's existence is no more due to the bright work of photosynthesis than to dark consorts with fungus beneath our feet.

Like the fungi we know by sight, endogone reproduces asexually by spores. But unlike the fruiting bodies of mushrooms, no winds buffet the roots of living trees. So, no breeze bears these spores to potential new sites for inoculation. As a substitute for wind, endogone trusts red-backed voles to carry its spawn where they will, likely, owing to the red-backed's forest affinity, to some similar and hospitable place.

When a vole eats a fungal fruiting body, it patters off to somewhere else, scattering feces like those I found in the urine-stained snow along its way, laced with gut-proof spores ready to sprout. A paper published in American Midland Naturalist, describing vole transport of fungal spores on the George Washington National Forest in Virginia, reported that scats from a red-backed vole collected over a two-week period held more kinds of fungal spores than human mycologists found in the same area in three years of careful collecting.

Forest ecologists believe this "seeding service" by red-backed voles is an indispensable part of forests' ability not only to live but to spread and reclaim lost sites. Without some vehicle to carry and "plant" underground spores, burned-over woods would remain burns, clearcuts would never grow back into woods, surface mines would forever be barren, and trees would never colonize farmland when it's abandoned. Investigations far more comprehensive and careful than Colleen's and mine found that red-backed voles were initially reluctant to cross "edges" into cuts, burns and surface mines but that they eventually do. These voles, then, can be thought of as something akin to subterranean bees, transporting spores of underground fungi, as true bees do with the pollen of flowering plants.

* * *

Going into the woods as I did that day on cross-country skis can be somewhat, I suppose, like cruising an ocean at high latitude. There are always icebergs about in those waters, yet we see only the exposed tip of something that's much bigger, hidden beneath the surface. By chance, I crossed paths with a red-backed vole in tormented death throes. I will never know what distress sent it spinning and circling among the gnarled stems of rhododendron and mountain laurel. I can ski more trails wondering if a weasel fang slashed its back as it flushed from some cairn, if some silent sickness lurks now inside vole skulls, or if cold alone stalked one lone vole that somehow lost track of its rock-and-root refuge. I will know, though, that a small rodent ushered my sight briefly beneath the surface, where, once in awhile, we get to sense the knotting of our own breath to all other living things.

Kettles of Grace

In early spring, then throughout summer, turkey vultures assemble and soar in flocks. Birders call them "kettles," sweeping, circling funnels of big birds. If you are fishing the Youghiogheny River or some parts of Laurel Hill Creek, you may see them appear over the canyon rim at mid-morning, one bird at a time, until there are 30 or more black buoyant beings orbiting over the gorge. Watching them is bad for the fishing. It erodes concentration the way the river has gnawed through the very ridges around you. But beholding their flight is a catch in its own right. It is a lesson in atmospheric topography, and it blunts the edge of unease about our own mortal course.

The vultures maneuver the gorge as kids on skateboards have mastered the concave half-pipe. They rise, effortless, over the hotter hillsides, then turn and fall into the cool, dank air above the stream. In the depth of the gorge, they must labor through the denser air, dragged along by its belly by the river itself. Here they pump and claw, their primaries splayed wide apart like the fingers of an ambitious pianist.

But you can see what's to come next if you pay attention. On the sun-soaked mountainsides, the oak leaves ripple and fan, their silver undersides winking in the updraft. The vultures toil toward the shoreline, plunge into the ascending columns and are born ever higher on the heat. There they assume their truest self, sweeping, silent wings held in their signature "V," uniform black save the metallic gray you can see through the trailing edge of the wings when the light is right.

It is interesting to be among people in the outdoors when vultures appear. If the birds are noticed at all, they will be called "hawks" by most observers. Tactfully point out the error, and your companions look stunned and surprised, as if vultures were mythic creatures or the inhabitants only of B-grade westerns.

They are real enough, and to tempt them I have sometimes lain on the ledges above the gorge in the searing sun, motionless as a living mammal can be, except for one eye squinting skyward to track the airborne birds in the event they would come too close. Their shadows leap and plummet across the treetops toward me. If they are far enough from the sun, I see the pink heads tilt a little in inspection as they pass over, but they never swing by for a second look. It is impossible to fool them. They know death too well, and they know a silly game when they see one.

Away they wheel and wander, in search of more trustworthy hosts where they find them. Their airy open patrols, in the bright light of day, across this familiar land where we live, is a sign that the end of life need be no dark stranger. It is the natural companion to living, no more to be feared than the breathing or the birth.

Fraxinus Lost

A reluctant dawn seeps above Laurel Ridge's stark silhouette. I'm in my threadbare chair beside the window and before the woodstove, where my coffee cup squats on the warming rack before accepting its bitter, enlivening brew. Yellow light beams through the stove's glass doors, burnishing every surface it strikes.

I'm glad for the heat and aroused by the light, but without the contentment I've long taken from burning wood in my home. This heat and light carry out of my stove the taint of loss. They are the heat and light of ash wood, and I may be among the last firewood burners on these ridges to bask in its bright combustion.

Yet, I accept this fire's tempered pleasure and burn all the ash I can; might as well. From what I see, and by the official word of the forestry bureau, every sizable ash across these slopes is dead, and though their wood has many qualities, durability after death is not among them. Even standing dead in the woods, as millions now do, ash succumbs fast to weather and rot. Either I burn this unwelcome glut now or see it decay into duff.

Ash's die-off happened so fast, across such an expanse, that it's unsettling. If you know our woods here, if you're attuned to their slow successional change and take reassurance in some degree of permanence there, it's terrifying. But to say that ash died off is not correct. Ash was done in by the emerald ash borer, a metallic-green beetle you'd be excused to mistake for a streamlined, space-suited grasshopper.

The emerald ash borer is a well-named but clandestine killer. The shiny-green beetles are harmless to an ash tree for the month or so, centered on

May; they exist as adults, except that females lay eggs in bark cracks and fissures. The translucent, grub-like larvae that hatch from those eggs, then burrow inward, are what wring life from an ash tree. They mine under the bark through the tender sapwood, boring serpentine tunnels that entomologists call galleries. If the invasion of larvae is dense enough, as it has been inside ash trees across the Ohio Valley hill country and the Alleghenies' western slope, the galleries intersect and overlap around the tree's circumference, looking like ancient runes, strangling the tree.

No emerald ash borer ever chewed through an ash trunk here before about 2005. *Agrilus planipennis* is native to China, whose northeastern forests are elegantly like our Appalachian woodlands, with analogous plants and insects that fit niches, fulfill roles we'd recognize from our own sylvan experience. The difference is that China's several ash species evolved in the ash borer's presence, devising biochemical defenses, enlisting allies to blunt and balance its crafty attack. As a sudden alien in North America, the borer faces no enemies here, so our ashes stand open to onslaught.

The borer spends more than 300 days out of sight, under the bark, in a furtive strategy that helped it get here, hitch-hiking inside the grain of ash-wood crates or palettes shipped in with imported, must-have merchandise—wide-screen TVs, perhaps. The first one identified in North America was caught among ash trees in a park in Canton, Michigan, near Lake Erie's western tip, in 2002. From there, the invasion exploded southward and east, engulfing urban groves along the Great Lakes, leap-frogging through Ohio Valley woodlots, and ascending the Alleghenies. Except for the epicenter in southern Michigan, no region became more saturated with emerald ash borers than our north-Appalachian uplands.

Depending on how finely you divide the taxonomy, either five or six ash species grow here, all of which belong to the genus Fraxinus—white, green, blue, black, red, and pumpkin ash. Red ash and green ash are genetic variants, sometimes considered the same species. Except for blue ash, which, like Asian ashes, manufactures tannin in its leaves so is less palatable to leaf-nibbling, egg-laying adults, all our ashes face the same internally girdled fate.

Green and white are our dominant ashes. They can be difficult to tell apart, but each has its favored conditions. Our western Allegheny foothills were "made for" green ash (*Fraxinus pennsylvanica*). Fast-growing, it likes sun and rich but well-drained soil and thrives, too, along the sinuous corridors of sluggish streams. Consider those habitat likes, then recall the most significant land-use change across hill-country Ohio, western Pennsylvania, and panhandle West Virginia since the mid-20th century—abandonment of farmland. Green ash has flourished here in the wake of old crop fields and pasture, surging up idled valleys and spreading over neglected hills.

White ash (*Fraxinus americana*) is a tree of upland forest, standing there with oaks and maples, and gains prominence over green ash as Allegheny ridges steepen and rise to the east. The blue ash (*Fraxinus quadrangulata*) can be found in those high woods, too, but is less common than white. Our other "minor" ashes claim limited niches in wetlands, on river islands, or floodplains. Given ash's prevalence here, wherever an adult emerald ash borer winged south from Michigan, it could land on an Appalachian ash tree.

I remember the first time I learned about the borer. It must have been around 2006 or '07. I'd seen—couldn't miss—a purple kite-like contraption, just bigger than my RFD mailbox, hanging in a tree in Ohiopyle State Park. I puzzled over the thing, then forgot it, but soon saw others, which prompted inquiry. These, I learned, were "prism traps" (the traps are triangular when viewed from either end), placed by the U. S. Dept. of Agriculture and the state Bureau of Forestry to monitor the emerald ash borer's initial advance into western Pennsylvania. Borers are drawn to purple color, and a pheromone lure inside the trap attracts adults to a sticky surface where they're caught and marooned. The purple snares were reassuring. "Well, at least we're on top of this early," I remember thinking. But no one, not even forest pest professionals, could envision the quiet ferocity of this invasion. Within three years of those traps' hanging to detect pioneers, ash trees around here declined, then died. Entomologists acknowledge now that because the borer larvae live beneath the bark for 11 months, grubs might have been mining through ash sapwood before the traps made their first capture.

Ash in mind and hand

Helplessness attends any attempt to describe a living ash tree's appearance—in the way that you can't summon up a friend's face after she has died. Peterson's Field Guide to Trees and Shrubs says ashes are tall trees of symmetrical form, with an oval crown and trunk that sub-divides low, a truth that can still be seen among the standing casualties. But look quick, as the decaying branches are falling away fast. Just give thought to where and how long you stop to rest in the woods on windy days.

A sure way to know an ash is to examine its juxtaposition of parts. All components of an ash tree are arranged as opposites. Twigs erupt opposite one another from larger branches, and the compound leaves likewise oppose their neighbor across the stem. All ashes have compound leaves, and even the leaflets are opposite their counterpart along the leaf's petiole. Ashes are our only tree whose leaves are both opposite and compound, so the dual verification is foolproof. Look close at a dead ash, stark and bare. This theme of opposites is easy to trace throughout its form.

Ash foliage, if I recall, had a lacy look in summer owing to its compound leaves. There is still time to learn to know the bark, though it, like the branches, is shedding away from the standing boles. On trees old enough to develop their signature pattern, the bark looks like parallel rows of steel chain running up the trunk. The "links" in the chains are ridges enclosing diamond-shaped basins. Examine the bark now, and you'll notice it's peppered with holes shaped like a "D," about the diameter of a pencil eraser. The "Ds" mark places where an adult beetle emerged from its larval gallery under the bark.

I see now that, before the borer, I never noticed how much ash was in the woods, how common it had been in its vigor. I'd walked among ash all my life, sat at their bases watching for deer, placed a hand upon them in passing without apprehending their spread. It's impossible now to overlook them. They stand out as pallid cadavers, peppered over with woodpecker pits, their bark sloughing off in 6-foot slabs, piling into spongey pyramids at the base. Somehow, I had tended to think of ash as a mid-size tree, rarely rivaling the big oaks or beeches. But now that they're gone, and that search-image of pallor and rot is ingrained in my brain, I stumble upon lifeless giants I'd failed to wonder at in their prime. What had preoccupied me so when I passed near this massive tree in the past? Is my mind capable of accommodating only the search for morels, or a deer's flicked ear, in a moment outdoors? Certainty that I would have admired these tall ashes had I known their end was near affords scant solace. So, I content myself with the warmth and light from their disassembly in my stove. I've made a ritual of it, a private homage.

When I awake and rekindle my fire, I feed the stove with ash splits only. I arrange the splits over the night's surviving coals, open the vent all the way, then sip coffee and study the burn unsullied by the flames of other fuel.

At my first sips, the coals dim as the added wood absorbs their heat, cooling the stove's interior. But before I'm halfway through the cup, the ash stack brightens at its base. Before I pour my second, flames are licking the undersides of lower splits. The ascending blaze kindles a slab, claims a foothold, then hops up to the next undersurface as if climbing a staircase from beneath.

Flames rising out of ash wood are yellow, clear, and steady. They never sputter, and they throw no sparks. My stove ticks and groans from its expanding parts but the wood burns quiet, as if it were a fuel for stoves first and, secondarily, the once-living tissue of a tree. As the splits torch, their flames burn uniformly across their lengths, with no flares like those that burst from black cherry. Those cherry flares erupt from pockets of resin trapped among the fibers. Ash's combustible molecules must be evenly spread along its grain without clumps or pockets, yielding this stable burn. Propane gas would behave this way, I imagine, if compressed into a bar I could carry and stack.

This steady burn may be linked in some molecular way to ash's quick surrender to the stroke of my maul. When I drive it down into a broad round of ash, the head burrows in with a satisfying cleave. Even if the round is too big to split in one blow, a straight rift shoots down the outside, and I'm encouraged. I know one more stroke will do it. I set myself, lift, drive, then torque my wrists on impact. The round vaults apart into two equal halves, with none of the tearing and shred characteristic of oak. Suddenly exposed, the new surface is the color of bread scarcely toasted.

Like all seasoned wood, ash has its own fragrance, strongest in the moment you rend it apart. Ash's scent is bright and clean. "Salt" comes to mind, but I'm not sure that's right, and the sense of salt is fleeting. If I press my nostrils to the new surface, I can prolong the aroma but not for long. It's pleasing but elusive, like stepping into a fresh-painted room you've returned to admire before your nose grows accustomed.

Ash wood is light for its volume and straight of grain, both traits long noted. "Fraxinus," the generic name for all ashes, translates in Latin as "spear" or "javelin," and the common name has roots in the old English "aesc," which meant "spear" or "lance." Light but strong, ash wood must have been prized as shafts for weapons that, for better or worse, shaped western civilization. I'll likely never wield an ash-shafted spear, but I can apprehend the qualities that lent this wood to that purpose. When I get my ash splits down to kindling size, I can grip the maul's handle close to the head and part the wood into springy strips with a flick of my wrist. The kindling leaps apart with pent-up strength that once begged some soldierly use.

Splitting ash down to kindling reveals another of this wood's qualities, less martial but equally prized. As my maul drives downward, a clear tone rings out from the parting bonds, oddly entertaining to hear. Sometimes, I give in to impulse and experiment with this tone, splitting pieces of varying sizes and wielding the maul at different rates to play a crude tune at my splitting stump, noting the pitch ascend as the strips grow smaller. I'm no musician, but when I learned that ash wood is prized for making electric-guitar bodies because of the way it enhances sound, I felt affirmed in this whimsy. If you attended a baseball game in the time before the borer, you've heard this signature ring from ash too. That gratifying "crack of the bat" pealed out of the spring of ash wood, long preferred for bats because its light weight allowed a batter's swing to achieve its highest velocity in the split-second his mind perceived the flight of the ball. Since the ash borer's march across mid-America, most bats are made from maple, hard wood, but it lacks ash's resilience. If you watch a game today, you'll notice how often maple bats explode in batters' hands.

After ash

A notable truth about life in modern America is that there is no general acknowledgment of indigenous ecological loss. Righteous angst simmers for rainforest and polar bears, but there is little heed to our own native fabric's unraveling. State highway departments sometimes fell dead ashes along roadsides, so a crashing ash doesn't impede the traffic, leaving the wood to lie in the ditch. That's about it. You could saw the trunks into manageable pieces to pick up and use (I do) if you dared risk stopping along the shoulder, offending the careening cars even by slowing down to exit the stream.

There is, however, an unconscious mourning apparent in every recent autumn. Weather forecasters, chambers of commerce, and tourism bureaus now annually note the "muted" fall foliage that disappoints visitors. Dry weather, wet weather, and late frost have all rationalized the deficient autumnal tint. But no voice ever proposes that the rapid disappearance of ash accounts for the drabness. Ash was dazzling in fall, wasn't it? Does memory serve me when I recall it as buttery-yellow, sometimes tinged around the edges with gauzy orange? Didn't it jump out to the eye, especially on overcast days? We may not have noted such radiance when it erupted before us every autumn, but we are aware of its absence, even if we cannot give a name to where it went.

Other repercussions go beyond the aesthetic. Landslides are part of this region's clay-soil geology and steep terrain. But these events are lately more frequent, complicating life around Pittsburgh's hilly perimeter. The television news reliably reports on these slides, noting frequent rains and saturated clay, both true enough. Video-feeds show the viscous mud, blocked highways, and teetering homes poised on the edge of suburban abyss. But never noted are jumbled piles of dead logs visible in many shots—ash logs to my eye—whose roots once knitted that hillside together and whose death surrendered the slope to gravity.

When today's children grow up without having known of ash trees, there will be an absence in their lives they have no way to sense. This strikes me as profound impoverishment, greater, perhaps than the vanishing of ash itself. I and all those my age have lived our lives in just that kind of vacuum left behind by American chestnut. Except for the stories and lore of "old-timers," I never knew this dominant climax tree of the Alleghenies, and I can't help but wonder what that void has meant in my life. But at least I knew that chestnut once lorded over these woods. Will children growing up today, in the wake of ash, even know such a lovely, useful tree once grew here in abundance? I can ask this question about children and ash because I did know ash in my time. I knew it direct and personal. I knew it connected to other things.

Ash in vivo

Sharp ridges wander across Greene County, Pennsylvania, embracing deep hollows in their weave, not unlike the chain-pattern of ash bark. Across many autumns, I would pick my way along the western slope of one such ridge, listening for the thrash of wild turkeys scratching in fallen leaves. A scatter of white ash grew among oaks and hickories across that slope. I knew where each stood and eased through the woods from one to the next, knowing I'd likely find a flock beneath one ash or another.

Hunting this way is sublime pleasure. You are always moving but slow enough to savor the fall woods' winey aroma, to feel on your fingertips the fine cellulose dust you can rub from the leaves' leathery gloss. By habit, I walk quiet in the woods, a challenge in dry leaves. As if by some grace, though, sounds of careful steps don't concern wild turkeys, especially if your gait is erratic, without the cadence of human ambulation. When scratching for a prized forage like ash seeds, turkeys make such a din themselves that an adroit hunter can approach a flock within shotgun-reach. When I'd done so, I liked to watch the birds awhile through the screening brush. I craved contact with their native, rural "rightness" in that place. Those birds belonged on that ridge, under the ashes. My deepest reward for hunting them well was the sense that I belonged there too.

After I'd watched the flock scratch and feed, I'd burst through the brush and run toward them at the best speed I could muster over rough ground, yelling, shooing, maybe firing off a shot in the air. The panicked turkeys sprinted and flushed in all directions, unleashing a riot of alarm "putts" to the tattoo of their stiff wings battering branches. As the birds escaped, a lingering shower of twigs and tendrils rained from the trees to affirm the chaos that had just happened, and I'd suck the chilled air for breath.

Such a disruption may seem odd, but scattering the flock is a tradition-al Appalachian way to hunt wild turkeys in the fall. In the days before game laws, when hill people hunted out of need, a skilled and patient hunter could kill most of a scattered flock in a long afternoon. While the woods settled, I'd wait a quiet quarter-hour, then stroke the wood-peg "striker" across the slate face of my call to fake a hen's assembly yelp. Social creatures, turkeys are desperate to regroup after such a fright, and if my calls rang true, unseen birds would yelp and "kee-kee" back from all directions. Soon, some would appear out at the limits of vision, dark and cautious, craning their necks, anxious to reassemble. And if I held motionless, they'd filter back onto the same scratched-up ground where I'd flushed them. Finally, I'd pick out one nice bird and end my hunt. So inclined, you could stay there for hours, calling more lonely birds back to the gun.

When I cleaned my prize for a feast, I'd open its crop, the pre-digestive pouch in the upper chest, to confirm what the birds had been eating. Each time I'd killed my turkey under an ash tree on that ridge, I could pull out a baseball-size wad of single-winged ash seeds, looking like the blades of canoe paddles— "samaras" in botanical terms—the bird had scratched for and swallowed.

Ashes were reliable seed-producers, which is why I could find a turkey flock on that ridge every fall. But in recent autumns, unless it's a good acorn year and the birds are scratching beneath oaks, the ridge is silent, with no thrash in the leaves up ahead, no scratched-up duff beneath the remains of skeleton ashes, and a diminished lure to be there.

Innocence, boon and hope

It may be no consolation that the rapid extermination of ash here is a case of ecological "what goes around comes around." The borer could never have spawned such hordes without a ubiquitous host, and ash could never have achieved the prominence it did across this region without radical alteration of the landscape by humans long before the borer hit. Ash's wholesale crash was set in motion two centuries earlier when settlers cleared the Ohio Country of its diverse forest cloak for farmland, laying the groundwork for widespread dominance by pioneer species like green ash when that same land was later abandoned. Once the invader benefitted from its welcoming jump-start in green ash, its fortified billions found and infested the other ash species.

Still, it is important to dispel any sense that the emerald ash borer "destroyed" North America's ash tree resource, even any hint of that sense this writing may have conveyed. The ash borer did nothing apart from what it evolved to do, which is to feed from an ash tree's inner membranes and reproduce itself. Our ash catastrophe was a matter of context, in which the borer obeyed its internal mandate suddenly free of all balancing checks on its abundance, in an altered place where its host had done much the same thing, dominating idled farmland at the expense of a more varied forest less vulnerable to borers, because it could. Unless we accept the borer's innocence in our loss, we remain ill-equipped to intercept other catastrophic invasions.

All living things exploit opportunity, which is why, in nature, a collapse can elicit a consequent boon. When I was a boy, following my father, uncles and their bird dogs across the boulder-strewn slopes above the Youghiogheny River to hunt ruffed grouse, which were abundant then, we sometimes were treated to the sight of an even more striking big bird, its wings flashing black and white in undulating flight among big trees. More often, we'd only hear its clamoring "Yuk, Yuk, Yuk" call from some unseen haunt. But rarely, this bird would alight on a trunk within sight, bigger than a crow, and I'd admire its rakish red crest, watch it hammering at the wood at a pace that seemed mechanistically rapid, not possible from a flesh-and-blood creature. My elders called it the "Indian hen," which seemed fitting to me then. Later, when I found that bird described in some periodical, likely Pennsylvania Game News, I learned it was the pileated woodpecker.

For years after those encounters, I read that the pileated woodpecker was in steep decline and feared its "laugh" would be resigned to my outdoor past. Ornithologists pronounced the pileated "old-growth obligate," that it needed extensive stands of mature timber to survive, especially the dead, cavity-riddled trees always present in mature forest. Wood-dwelling insects thrive in such habitats, which woodpeckers excavate and devour. But, experts observed, forests extensive and old enough to sustain the big woodpecker were disappearing or being fragmented into smaller blocks, and the bird would vanish from American woods within a human generation.

Yet, if you go into any tract of woods in our region today, even woodlots that checker farm regions, even suburbs with trees, you are likely to see or hear pileated woodpeckers. Their numbers grew, and their range ballooned over the past decade in response to the numberless ash borer larvae they pluck from tunnels with a few raps at the decaying wood. In what's left of the ash woods you can hear their drumming from all directions, and the ground is littered with punky chips they've carved out with their beaks, leaving rectangular excavations along the trunks. Cavity nesters, pileated woodpeckers find perfect nest sites in the pocked trees.

Even with their populations spiking, woodpeckers can't eat enough of the larvae to make a difference for ash, and the woodpecker irruption is likely temporary, a wave of birds following a wave of abundant forage.

I like to think about that image of a living wave because within it glimmers a hint of hope for ash. Hope, even if baseless, is, in our time, an alluring refuge for those attuned to the natural world.

No apparent pattern explains where this occurs, but at "random" places in or near dead ash woods, you will, even today, come upon stands of ash seedlings, high as your knees and dense as weeds. Sometimes these clumps crowd beneath the gray remains of their parents. In other places, no adult ashes are present, indicating that the massed deposit of wind-borne samaras blew in on the same gust together and found suitable footing. Born of the last fruiting by lingering ashes, these natal clusters stand lanky as ginseng stalks, too gaunt to attract a female borer intent on egg-laying and with too little girth to harbor larvae. They are hard to spot in winter, but in summer, the pale-green compound leaves betray them, beckoning you to check closer for their opposite orientation of leaflet, leaf, and twig, which proves them to be what you hoped. Once your eye learns to spot these seedlings, you'll notice others, and your hope that ash trees may yet be part of our place here will soar.

A tempting prospect leaps to mind when you encounter such a trove. Maybe the ash borer will over-achieve here, eat itself out of existence. Maybe, with all the ash trees big enough for a borer to bore killed by its own mastication, it will die out for lack of hosts and be gone. Then, these persevering seedlings could grow unmolested, mature and loose their own seed to the wind.

That may be a naïve vision, rooted less in rationality than in yearning. I have read no ecologists' judgments on this possibility, and when I encounter some informed treatise so directed, I may likely avoid its conclusions. I'd rather be able to hold onto hope.

Hurricanes, Turkeys, and Amphibians

In the woods that cloak the Allegheny ridges, the most abundant of living things can be, literally, underfoot. Yet, despite their great numbers, these wild legions are seldom seen. That's true of the redback salamander (*Plethodon cinereus*), proclaimed by herpetologists to be, perhaps, the most plentiful vertebrate animal in Appalachia. Herpetological literature tells me that thousands of these amphibians may live within a few hundred yards of my house. But it took a hurricane and a wild gobbler to reveal the redback salamander up close.

Redback salamanders live in moist deciduous woodlands from maritime Canada south to North Carolina and westward throughout the Great Lakes states and provinces to northern Minnesota. They are slender animals, reaching almost four inches in length from snout to tail tip. Females average larger.

The more you learn about this salamander, the more you suspect it was named before the study of the animal was well underway. Though most individuals are aptly named for the broad, brick-red stripe extending from the base of the head to halfway down the tail, not all redbacks have a red back. Some are gray across the back; some are entirely black, lacking the conspicuous stripe. Across much of the redback's range, all the forms can be found together, although there are regional differences in the proportions of red-striped, gray-backed, and black-backed specimens.

Oddly, the rugged Allegheny plateau of southern Potter County, Pennsylvania, and the gentle inland coast of Lake Erie in northeastern Ohio are known to harbor an all-red (erythristic) form. Because those distinct landscapes are starkly different from one another but not so far apart, many herpetologists believe the all-red redback is more widespread but has, somehow, eluded searchers elsewhere.

Redbacks are entirely terrestrial, making their home in leaf litter and under rocks and decaying logs, always seeking a balance between wet and dry. They need the moisture held within humus and decaying leaves but shun standing water. Like all the lungless salamanders living in Appalachia, they breathe through their skin. Breathing while immersed in water is as impossible for a redback salamander as it is for a horse. Actually, it's more so; a horse could breathe with its snout above the surface. But to carry out respiration, a lungless salamander, such as the redback, needs to have its skin exposed to humid air.

In summer's heat and drought, redbacks seek cool dampness underground. They use worm channels or the excavations of small mammals like voles or shrews to reach better conditions. Scientists have found redbacks as deep as one meter beneath the leaf litter. But soaking rain summons the necessarily opportunistic redbacks back up to the surface to forage or, in mid- to late-autumn, to court, mate, and lay their eggs.

Winter finds them using the same underground haunts to escape freezing, but only briefly. As amphibians go, redback salamanders are tolerant of cold. They may remain active into December and are known to begin their spring emergence by the end of January. During mild spells in mid-winter, they may clamber about beneath rocks and roots while snow lies thick above them.

I had encountered redbacks at random a few times over spans of years. When I uncovered a couple of redbacks while cutting fallen oak logs for firewood, I looked them up in Peterson's Field Guide to Reptiles and Amphibians and read enough to recognize the eponymous red-backed form. But I'd known almost nothing else about them until Hurricane Sandy roared over the mountains, her torrents of rain chilling into a blizzard across the ridges.

Sandy struck in late October, during the fall turkey hunting season in Pennsylvania, coinciding with the redback salamander's peak of courtship.

The storm's predicted approach delayed my normal obligations and offered a chance to hunt. Hunting wild turkeys in the fall feels more like true hunting than pursuing the birds in the more celebrated spring season. Fall turkey hunting demands knowledge of the landscape—where wild grapes grow, where acorns and beechnuts fall to ground, and where tall, sheltered trees offer good night-time roost sites. In fall, the birds' behavior is driven by food. Predicting where turkeys will feed, travel, and roost in the autumn woods is, to me, more satisfying than calling sex-struck gobblers in spring.

That Monday morning of Sandy's arrival, I started out with a different plan, driving west, out of the mountains, through the wind and darkness toward a lowland ridge on the far side of the Monongahela where I often hunt. But rain lashed the windshield with such force that I turned around, climbed back over the mountain, and retreated to bed—for me, an uncommon surrender. My revised plan was to enjoy another hour of warm, dry sleep, then hunt in the highlands, where it would be easier to get back inside by the fire.

The storm itself hinted where turkeys would be. Here, on the inland margin of that swirling eye, the gusts roared out of the northwest, tossing the treetops and driving rain sideways against the trunks. Conditions suggested the flocks would be somewhere on a southeast slope, shielded from the worst gusts. And if the turkeys sensed what was coming over the next two days, they'd be cramming their crops while they could, with whatever food they could find.

I sought out such a place and found turkey sign right away. The day-old scratchings amid the oak leaves told that turkeys had fed on acorns the day before. There, surrounded by sign on the lee side of the ridge felt like a logical place to set up.

A jumble of downed logs offered concealment. I settled in where I could watch the scratchings and draped a camo raincoat over my lap. Rain pounded the trees so hard that trickles of white "suds" drained down the trunks. You only see that when it's been raining hard for a long time. I've never heard an explanation for it, but my guess is that a long hard downpour leaches oils out of the bark and forms a bubbly emulsion—like soap film that flows down a shower curtain.

I sat there for a couple of hours, squinting through the deluge. Reluctant to expose my slate call to the rain, I cast out occasional hoarse yelps from a mouth call. Finally, the dark shapes of four turkeys appeared around the hill's shoulder. They were all mature gobblers, picking their way toward the same spot where they'd scratched in the leaves the day before, their long beards swaying with their strides. Farther down the hill, another half-dozen turkeys emerged from the gloom.

Watching wild turkeys feed in the woods is enlightening and entertaining. It shows why turkeys successfully find a diverse diet across a wide range of woods, swamp, and savannah throughout much of North America. They stalk over the ground like miniature biped dinosaurs, placing their feet with deliberate intent, one after another, as they peer down for some sign of a productive place to probe. Spotting some clue, they spread their scaly toes and scratch powerfully at the leaf litter with a leg's full swing. Leaves, humus, and debris spray out behind them in a dark organic cloud as they expose the bare soil across a crude triangle, ten or so inches across at its base, tapering to a point in the direction the bird is facing. An observant turkey hunter can trail a feeding flock by noting the orientation of the birds' scratchings in the leaves. Noise can draw an attentive hunter, too. When two dozen turkeys scratch in dry autumn leaves, occasionally gobbling, yelping, or clucking to one another, the cacophonous racket is not something you expect to hear in tranquil woods.

At times the birds will scratch rapidly with alternate feet, the way a dog digs with its front paws, or they'll hop up and down while using both feet at once to broaden the excavation, like a huge rufous-sided towhee. When they're satisfied with their effort in that spot, not a leaf lies on the barren scar they've raked, but a patchwork of rootlets, seeds, hulls, insects, and other potential food items lay unearthed.

Once a turkey has a spot exposed, it examines the bare earth, turning its head side-to-side to bring both eyes into play. Then come exploratory pecks, the beak turning over items and picking others up for testing. When the bird locates something edible, it gulps and swallows.

These four gobblers scratched, peered, and pecked their way right into shotgun range as I'd hoped, and I watched them long enough to select the biggest of the dark quartet. A downed wild turkey doesn't look so regal and impressive when its feathers are matted and soaked, but hefting that big wet tom out of the woods brought the satisfaction of knowing I had endured the storm's early ravages and could soon get dry.

The gobbler hung in the chill of my shed for a couple of days as the rainstorm morphed into a blizzard. Sixteen inches of dense wet snow fell in a day-and-a-half, shredding hemlock trees and matting down thickets. When I took the bird down for plucking, I got an unexpected insight into the predatory interactions that go on all the time in the woods.

Among all gallinaceous, ground-dwelling birds, an expandable blad-der-like sac, known as the "crop" sits at the base of the throat atop the breast. The crop holds food before it is passed to the muscular gizzard, inside which are bits of stone, sand or shell the bird has ingested to serve as abrasives. The crop is a buffer against bad weather and long nights when a turkey can't fuel its fast metabolism with constant feeding. It enables turkeys, grouse, pheasants, quail, and their cousins to forage heavily when conditions permit, storing more than enough food to meet the bird's im-mediate needs. Later, if a storm, darkness, or deep snow prevents feeding, the cached food passes continuously to the gizzard for grinding and the beginning stages of digestion.

When crammed with food, the crop's smooth membranous surface is stretched tight and appears translucent. In strong light, you can see a suggestion of what's inside. Squeezing a bird's full crop also yields clues to its contents. If you have some familiarity with what you might be feeling there, you can sense the curved contour of beechnuts inside or recognize the rub of acorns against one another through the gauze-like tissue. This turkey's crop bulged almost to the bizarre. It was distended to the girth of a grapefruit, with bumpy knots where the points of acorns pushed outward against membranous constraint.

I cut a slit in the taut crop with my pocketknife, and the sweet, warm scent of fermenting vegetation rose around my nostrils. The mass inside revealed a record of the bird's whereabouts and dietary choices during the last hours of its life. Crammed together were about 50 red oak acorns, dozens of wild cherry pits, fragments of what looked like black walnut (how do wild turkeys crack a walnut shell?), a mass of small leaves and fern tips, some unidentified segmented worms and, most surprisingly, eleven intact salamanders.

The salamanders, of course, were long dead, but since a turkey doesn't chew, they were in perfect condition except for a spreading pallor across the skin. They showed no outward trauma from being dug up from under the leaves and swallowed whole by a 20-pound bird. Their limbs entwined with fern leaves, and their tails encircled acorns. With the knife point, I sorted them out and lined them up on the snow while I plucked their killer clean for roasting.

Most of the salamanders carried the brick-red stripe down the middle of the back, but a few were all gray. Otherwise, they all looked alike. Their uniform size, the precise taper of the tails and snouts, their slender shape, the positions of the costal grooves along their sides and their mottled "salt-and-pepper" bellies marked all eleven as redback salamanders. There on the snow lay a sampling of at least two of the species' color forms.

Hurricane Sandy had freed me to hunt, and she set the turkey and the salamanders up for an encounter at a time when each had to seize the moment for different reasons.

The wild gobbler I'd shot had to feed before the weather worsened. Within hours it had gorged on foods you can often find in a turkey's crop. Few references cite amphibians as turkey food, but this gobbler had also found and consumed 11 salamanders. What a protein boost that must provide to a big bird stoking its high-strung metabolism against the uncertain ravages of a mountain storm.

The swallowed redbacks had obeyed an imperative of their own. Before Sandy's arrival, the fall had been dry. The salamanders had likely been aestivating somewhere deep beneath the soil, waiting for rain to commence their mating. Sandy summoned them up in a critical window before the onset of winter, just as wild turkeys obeyed a heightened need to forage hard.

Published descriptions of redback behavior report that during the fall mating season, male-female pairs establish a territory and stay close together but avoid other pairs. That intra-specific avoidance suggests that the turkey picked up the salamanders at different locations rather than in one windfall find. Since wild turkeys don't feed at night, the bird must have found and eaten all 11 salamanders earlier that same morning. And nine other turkeys were visible to me when I killed the gobbler, all of which, it seems safe to assume, were finding and eating redback salamanders at the same astonishing rate, supporting scientists' observations of the redback's singular abundance in woods like these.

Herpetologists are doubtless less proficient at finding salamanders than a wild turkey, but even they have documented redbacks at impressive densities. The greatest concentration recorded is 2.8 redbacks per square meter, found at Mountain Lake Biological Station in western Virginia. If that same density continued over an area with the dimensions of a football field, close to 12,000 redbacks might live between the end zones. Even at lower densities elsewhere, researchers believe the total biomass of redback salamanders in woodlands across the Alleghenies exceeds that of all birds (that assertion seems questionable if a flock of wild turkeys happens across the hypothetical acre) and equals the biomass of small mammals.

It is reassuring but a little surprising to learn of such native natural abundance in our current time. We're more accustomed to hearing about large numbers of destructive exotics that threaten to shred the weave of our native webs. Snakeheads, pythons, feral hogs, Japanese knotweed, gypsy moth, Asian carp, and hemlock woolly adelgid, unchecked and hell-bent on expansion, are the out-of-place hordes that dominate our attention. A 4-inch native salamander crawling copiously over the hills is nice to ponder. But the redback's encouraging abundance should be viewed in perspective.

The redback salamander is only one of 76 species of salamanders that share at least parts of its range. Appalachia is the birthplace of the salamander tribe worldwide, and the mountains still hold the planet's greatest diversity of salamander species.

Importantly, among Appalachian salamanders, the redback is a generalist. It lives in a broad range of forest types and utilizes, like the wild turkey, a diverse diet of its own, so it needs no specialized habitat features, such as rock cliffs or spring seeps. Occupying a large range and existing in varying conditions, redbacks can absorb some degree of change and yet survive as a species. As long as hardwood forests of varying composition receive periodic rain, the redback thrives. Most other mountain salamanders are far more specialized. They live across smaller ranges and find their food, mating sites, and shelter within a narrow range of constraints. To them, change is more threatening, and change is everywhere in the mountains today.

A gathering of experts at the Appalachian Salamander Conservation Workshop at Front Royal, Virginia, in 2008 agreed that most amphibian populations, including salamanders, have declined worldwide in recent decades. Long-term studies indicate that 38 species of lungless salamanders in Appalachia have declined by as much as 50 percent during the 1990s.

Many possible causes are noted. Climate change may be affecting some salamanders with restrictive temperature and humidity demands and without the redback's ability to wait out poor conditions underground. Invasive species, including disease and fungi, have reduced others. Energy production, including mountain-top removal coal mining, natural gas drilling, pipeline construction, wind energy facilities on ridge-tops, roads, residential development, and other rapid changes that fragment woodland into smaller, and often drier, patches impacts others.

No proceedings, papers or scientific meetings cite wild turkeys as a threat to salamander diversity and abundance, and likely they are not, even though turkey flocks have grown and expanded greatly across the region during the same period that salamanders have declined. Still, my observation after a turkey hunt is a strong sign that turkeys would certainly eat whatever salamanders they happened across, rare or not.

It's my sense that I found what I did because the behavioral idiosyncrasies of wild turkeys and redback salamanders, in response to a late-autumn storm, juxtaposed the two in a way that enabled turkeys to capitalize on the redbacks' determined emergence.

That wild turkeys consume salamanders when they can is not necessarily cause for conservationists' alarm. But neither is the abundance of one particular kind of salamander proof that all is well in the woods. We see clearly only slim fragments of what goes on among the wild in our own daily lives. Sometimes, something improbable like a turkey hunt in a hurricane opens a portal, and we perceive a little more than normal. But it's just a little more illumination. The real story is still out there, on a course that we may or may not have nudged this way or that. Knowing that is a start.

Sylvatica: Coldest Animal in the World

The phrase "If it quacks like a duck . . ." reveals something about a cavalier user. It proves the speaker has never sat motionless for two hours next to a puddle in the woods at the end of winter, waiting for wood frogs to reappear and resume their calling. This I have done, and because of it, I avoid flippant use of the "quacks like" axiom.

Not always would I have shied from that saying. Far back in our youth, friends and I, eager for spring, hiked downstream along Dunbar Creek to its confluence with the Youghiogheny River. Dunbar Creek courses through a deep, rocky ravine, but as the flow nears the river, the hills fall away, and the flow twists upon itself as if resisting union with the river. At the outsides of bends are mucky flats where, in early spring, the mild stench of skunk cabbage stabs at your nostrils and where the creek spills over at high flow, flooding the woods. As the floods recede, the retreating creek leaves behind puddles marooned among the trees.

As we hiked downstream, somewhere along that corridor, a clamor like quacking ducks rose from behind a rise of silt that flanked the creek. We crept close, planning to flush the whole flock for the thrill of it.

From the crest, we sprang, but there was no tumult of wings, no urgent ascent. Our intrusion caused only a furtive stirring across the stranded pool, and silence. The quacking had been raucous, loud and near, yet no living thing departed the pool. What, we marveled, had we heard?

Later, our return traced the same route, and we were amazed to find the clamor resumed. Stealth then seemed wiser than all-out assault. We inched upward and slid our gaze over the swell of ground and across the now shadowy strip of swamp. There, over that entire puddle, long and broad as a railroad car, squirmed a dense mat of frogs.

The pond's surface could have been the knotted and warty skin of some huge cold-blooded creature. Paired humps of frog eyes, by the hundreds, rumpled that skin, and kicking, stroking, swimming frogs swelled it at random. Still more frogs tussled and jousted. Pairs clambered over one another. Tandems of two or more clung together. Some clumps were trios, the rearmost clawing to dislodge the grip of the frog before it. At first, these knotted frogs appeared to be fighting, but even pre-adolescents sense that such grappling comes out of carnal intent. And over all the clambering throbbed that same garrulous quacking we'd heard there before.

Recovering from our awe, we began to watch individual frogs rather than the mass and saw that the sides of the heads of some pulsed and bulged with the cacophony that drowned out even the flow of the creek.

That watery riot, we learned later, was a colony of wood frogs rapt in their ancient, annual procreative rite. The "quacking" was the mating call of the males, produced by forcing air from the paired vocal sacs that swell before each note, like life-preservers, at the sides of the head. The din rising from a breeding pool sounds like anything but the croaking sounds we link with frogs. My young friends and I took the noise for quacking ducks. Others who have heard it for the first time have mistaken it for the angry cawing of crows, squawking out their assembly call as when, as a flock, they assault a hawk.

Though not often noticed, wood frogs inhabit an enormous and irregularly shaped range fit to forest and to cold. The Allegheny Mountains of western Pennsylvania, where my friends and I disturbed their mating, are nearly the southeastern extreme of the species' reach, anchoring an outlying prong that follows hemlock and hardwoods south along the Appalachians. Otherwise, the wood frog is a northern animal, quacking goodbye to winter from central Alaska, southeast across Canada's spruce-fir interior to the Great Lakes and New England, and northeast over the Quebec muskeg to the Labrador Sea.

Rana sylvatica is moderate in size among the frogs, averaging about two-and-a-half inches in length from snout to vent. Females are larger than males and can exceed three inches. The wood frog's unmistakable mark is the "robber's mask," a darkish to black swath reaching from the snout along the side of the head, over the eye, to beyond the "ear" or tympanum. The mask is always visible, despite the wide variety of background color that wood frogs exhibit, ranging from pinkish to almost black.

Once, years after that first encounter, I saw a wood frog wear two different colors within a span of minutes. An abandoned mountain homestead had decayed into duff, leaving behind the hand-dug cellar that filled each spring with rain, melted snow and mating wood frogs. The pool was dark organic mire at the bottom, and every frog in it was dark in color, matching the background. As I lay there, stretched out and watching, a wood frog hopped past my elbow from out of the woods on its way to join the others. The latecomer paused for a time, only inches from my nose, and I could plainly see its black mask in contrast against the lighter head. The rest of the body was light tan, like khaki pants.

A few more jumps carried the frog into the water, where I watched it closely. It sat motionless on the muck while other frogs gamboled and clambered about, clutching at females and pushing away rivals. In about the time it takes to read a couple of these paragraphs, the newcomer changed from pale-tan to near-black, matching the skin of every other frog at the site.

Life for a wood frog in a northern forest scarcely resembles the familiar image of bullfrogs lazing in the warm shallows of southern sloughs. These frogs are active terrestrial predators, hunting night or day for forest insects from the time they leave the breeding ponds in early spring until their uniquely extreme hibernation begins in the fall. During that active season, a wood frog may forage over several acres of woods. Their bodies are built for overland travel, with a narrow athletic trunk, long, muscular hind legs, and front-foot "fingers that are unwebbed but well developed. The dark eye "mask," herpetologists believe, camouflages the distinct dark pupil, which might otherwise alert predators or prey.

In The Frog Book, Mary C. Dickerson described some of the species' adaptations to terrestrial existence:

Land-life, and the broader experience resulting therefrom, seems to have produced a somewhat higher development in this frog. It not only looks much more intelligent, but it is certainly less unintelligent in some of the ways of its living, than other frogs. It jumps farther than most of the others, and has the habit of turning during the movement, so that when it strikes the ground it is facing the enemy. It is much more alert in getting food, resembling the toad in this respect. It sees the moving insect at a distance of several feet, stealthily walks or creeps toward it, and perhaps follows it some distance, before making the capture.

Its dry-land lifestyle allows the wood frog to exploit a vast territory with scant competition from other frogs. No other frog species, for instance, live north of the Arctic Circle. But like all frogs and toads, wood frogs are wedded to water once each year and must obey the reproductive imperative shared by all amphibians. To stake their northern terrestrial advantage, wood frogs had to not only develop a body form that favors land travel but also acquire the linked abilities to survive cold winters and to breed fast in temporary springtime pools where standing water is otherwise scarce.

The wood frog's answer to cold is unlike any other northern animal that shares its sprawling range. Most birds fly away from cold; others fluff insulating feathers, or roost within snow itself to hold onto heat. Woodchucks excavate below the freeze, and most frogs go torpid in pond bottom mud. The wood frog's response is simpler—in every aspect but biochemical. No one knows exactly when or by what trigger, but sometime each autumn, perhaps when frosts fall on successive mornings, each wood frog wriggles into a shallow, solitary burrow beneath some leaves wherever it happens to be in the woods and, as the cold deepens, freezes solid.

Scientists otherwise disinterested in frogs but bent on sending human travelers across space to other worlds have studied this unique (among vertebrates) wood frog feat. They've described what happens but cannot explain how the molecules involved "know" what to do and when. Their descriptions boil down to this: As the wood frog hunts down and tongue-spears insects all summer—many of which, themselves, would otherwise freeze under some shred of bark or leaf fold—it caches glycogen, in huge amounts, in its liver. Glycogen is the universally stored form of carbohydrate. When ice begins to form on the wood frog's skin, the glycogen breaks into the simple sugar, glucose. The frog's heart, then, pumping feverishly to keep ahead of its own hardening, floods the muscles and other organs in a massive and concentrated glucose bath. Once delivered throughout the body, the glucose "cryoprotectant" enables cells to freeze and thaw without the damage otherwise caused by the change of liquid water to ice and back again. Such extreme and sustained sugary saturation is unknown otherwise among vertebrates. Endocrinologists do know, though, that bloodstream insulin, which regulates a wood frog's carbohydrate metabolism, is radically different from the insulin within a bullfrog, which, if once frozen, would never utter another croak. Even a wood frog's brain and blood freeze during winter's depths, prompting some who have studied its seasonal sleep to call it "the coldest animal in the world."

Later, as winter relents, the frozen, sugar-soaked frog does not thaw uniformly, like a popsicle would do left to melt in the sun. The frog "melts" in reverse-order from which it froze. The heart, liver and blood thaw first, working together to resume the glucose bath until the muscles, skin and skeleton become, once again, pliant, living tissue.

Had I known all that forty-some years after the quacking along Dunbar Creek fooled my friends and me, I may not have deliberately disrupted another, though smaller, frog orgy atop Laurel Mountain.

The mid-March sun was bright at late morning. The crest of the ridge stands a long way from permanent water, and the quacking was both a surprise and a delight. It seemed to rise a long way off through the woods, but I reached the scant puddle quickly by tracking the sound. The pool covered about the area of a parked car and may have been six inches deep at its center. With no stream near, it had to be a remnant of rainstorms over the mountain's clay soil. Its water was clear as air over a bottom of matted grass and leaves, and already a softball-size mass of jelly-encased eggs spread to the sun in the depths.

Just as I parted ironwood brush to peer at the pond's occupants, the surface gave a slight shudder, and the quacking ceased, as the puddle along Dunbar Creek had "reacted" decades before.

I wanted to watch the love-struck frogs in action but had scared them into hiding, so decided to wait them out. They had, after all, only so much time to complete their task. If I stayed hidden, silent and still long enough, I reasoned, they would reappear.

The ironwood spread itself near one end of the puddle, with enough high ground at its roots so that I could sit, dry, and lean back against the bifurcated bole in relative comfort. I had in my daypack a camouflage jacket and mask that I use in the later spring to hunt wild turkeys. These I put on and settled the furrow of my back over the ironwood's muscular bumps.

Ten minutes passed, attested by the watch I could see by pushing back the jacket's camo-cuff, then 20, and then a half-hour. The sun wheeled a few degrees, and ravens gabbled somewhere off behind me. A troop of chickadees and titmice passed through, some lingering to inspect ironwood buds. But no frogs stirred.

Relative comfort, of course, is just that, relative to less comfort, and as I sat there, motionless, comfort drained away. It is interesting, and perhaps it explains something about our own human drive to move and explore, how 200 pounds of flesh, bone and blood can, after a time, bear down on one point where some irregular hump of earth or bark confronts a cluster of neural receptors. Through that point, you become aware of your own weight. The earth's gravity, then is no mere concept. It feels exactly like the vector it is, pulling at your mass in one direction, focused as a lens does to sunlight, through that inconvenient hump to the planetary center. Concealed there, I weighed the absurdity of a large, distracted mammal trying to wait out an amphibian that can freeze solid for five months. And in the lengthening absence of frogs, I wondered if, perhaps, they could sense my heartbeat—12 or 15 feet away—pulsed through my pained butt cheeks, then on through the sodden soil around them.

But after 40 minutes, two points of glinting light showed atop a bulge, no broader than a thumbnail, at the puddle's margin. At the same inconvenient moment, a yawn rose in my throat, and I drew in a sighing breath, half again greater than my normal volume at rest. The frog, I am certain, sensed it, and the bulge sank and was gone. But we'd crossed some threshold in this waiting, those frogs and I. Urgency must have outweighed caution because, over the next ten minutes, more bulges appeared over the puddle's surface and around its edge. Before an hour had passed, I could see a dozen pairs of eyes, sometimes even the dark masks of frogs with their heads just barely in the air.

I sensed but could not be sure all the first reappearing frogs were females. Some were poised on the matted grass. Others floated in open water, their hind legs splayed and waiting. Perhaps they felt, stronger even than the ardor of the males, a seasonal window closing, the need to get those eggs laid and the tadpoles grown before their puddle dried up in the strengthening sun.

More bulges arose on the surface and more arrow-point heads popped out of the grass. They were showing up in clusters. Each time I looked to a new part of the puddle I saw a frog that hadn't been there. A palpable tension was rising, a communal tautness, something like a ticking clock sensed faintly in an adjacent room at the depth of a sleepless night. The eyes of the nearer frogs were moving inside their sockets, casting their gaze over new sectors at each tick of that "clock." Searching for me? For other frogs?

As more frogs appeared, little blurts of vibration spread out on the surface from around some of their heads, and I thought they were about to call. Still, the silence persisted. Finally, there came one timid "cluck," not unlike the alarm "putt" of a wild turkey when it has grown suspicious of a hidden hunter. Then came a more confident "quack," then another, and finally, in sudden communal climax, the whole colony began to quack, splash, kick and clamber over one another. This was about 100 minutes after I'd begun my vigil, a long time to frogs whose future has to be forged in a few brief days.

Those frogs may as well have saved their sudden eruption of ardor for later because once I'd witnessed their resurgence, it was time for me to move. With my first awkward rustle, the puddle shuddered as every frog dove again into hiding, and the woods were quiet under the sun.

Thinking back over other encounters with breeding wood frogs, some colonies I "discovered" have been less timid in my prying presence. Some, I could walk up next to the pool in plain view while the frogs continued their rite in oblivion. Perhaps it was just that I observed those colonies at a later point in the process when the whole aggregation was so near to some point of no-return that there was no stopping the urge, not even in the interest of self-preservation.

That may well be, for water, to a wood frog, is fleeting. From the snow-melt of Arctic tundra to soggy floodplains along Appalachian streams, wood frog reproduction depends on standing water that won't stand long. That may be why wood frogs freeze solid so near the surface of the ground, to give them a "jump-start" on getting out and active to find an acceptable puddle and other frogs at the earliest opportunity.

Breeding in temporary "vernal" pools not only relieves the wood frog of competition from other frogs, it generally isolates wood frogs from predation by fish, though they are sometimes eaten by mink, raccoons and some birds of prey that find the breeding masses. I used the word "generally" because of something I saw along Clark's Creek, which parallels the Appalachian Trail for several miles across central Pennsylvania. The creek had inundated its floodplain, then receded, but a 14-inch brown trout had swum out of the main channel and into a streamside puddle and become imprisoned there when the creek shrunk back to normal flow. That trout swam among a mass of wood frogs with two webbed wood frog feet sticking out the sides of its mouth. During the couple of hours I watched the fish cruise the pool, it made no progress in getting the frog further down its gullet. Nor did it ever attempt to expel its obstructed meal.

Congregation at the breeding pools begins with the first several consecutive nights when the temperature remains above freezing. In the mountains of West Virginia, wood frog breeding has been reported as early as February 20. Researchers have found that most wood frogs, but not all, return to their natal pool to breed. Others, for some reason, find new mating pools. To find suitable water, they must track subtle changes in humidity, follow the smell of water, simply head downhill, or home in on the calls of other wood frogs to join new colonies.

Often, ice still covers much of the pool when breeding begins and returning cold snaps can rime the pond with a new ice layer. Undeterred by cold, of course, the frogs simply retreat to the bottom and await permanent thaw.

Once at it in earnest, wood frogs keep up the frantic breeding, in which the male clasps the larger female from behind and sheds sperm over her spewing eggs, for one to two weeks. Females lay two to three thousand eggs, each punctuated by a dark central nucleus, in gelatinous masses. Late-laying females deposit their egg masses on and around those laid before, forming large globular "reefs" on woody debris and the pond bottom.

Considering the brief availability of their breeding water, compressed as it is between winter's reluctant surrender and the desiccating summer sun, the wood frog frenzy at vernal pools is understandable. Eggs laid first, at the center of the communal mass, are warmer, better protected from late freezes, and hatch sooner. A tadpole that hatches sooner enjoys better odds at maturing and hopping away as a fully-formed frog before the pond dries up, passing on the genes of its more aggressively amorous parents. Across the eons, selection has favored frogs that cast aside caution over those that stayed hunkered down in hiding when some predator passed.

The wood frogs quacking and clambering in pools, puddles and tundra thaw-water now, in our time, were born out of that abandon. What an odd existence—frozen solid for months, to awaken in torrid proliferative furor, and then to close the circle hunting bugs for half a year in dry land forests. But the earth offers up what it will in conditions, niches and risk. *Rana sylvatica*, in our human way of seeing, is a pioneer, an explorer, probing out at the edge of hospitable places, throbbing quiet woods back to life with a joyful quack. Leading all other life into spring.

Encountering 'cats

To my knowledge, you cannot plan a bobcat encounter. For one thing, they're cats, unpredictable, mercurial cats. Bobcats live in rough places at low densities across big home ranges. One might suppose they even have a hard time locating one another, by calls and by scent, at their species' crucial annual time.

But I've been lucky; that and perhaps I've logged enough woods time to allow for random crossings of paths.

Once, imprudently, I was cross-country skiing in a place not well suited to having long slats clamped to your feet. I skirted the margin of a ledge that looms over a 40-foot drop to jumbled talus, facing a yawning expanse of woods to the west. Mountain laurel grows dense there, so I must have been making noise. But as I pushed out onto snow-mantled rock, I surprised a bobcat in broad daylight on the precipice lip. We looked at one another from 20 yards, but the cat's eye's betrayed no alarm. Instead, it seemed to be forming a plan. Pinned as it was against the cliff, it could not retreat, so it streaked by within reach of my ski pole, then disappeared in rock-voids and crevices farther along the outcrop.

Another time we were camped on a trout stream, enjoying that settled-in span after a meal and before eyes staring into campfire embers begin that droop toward sleep. There came a sudden stirring, a rush beyond the firelight. Before we could add up the clues, a rabbit dashed through the waning circle of firelight between us, pursued by a bobcat matching its desperate feints. Moments later, squeals from the darkness told the chase's outcome.

More recently, hot and winded, I rested near the foot of a waterfall, watching its flume and close enough to be cooled by its enveloping spray. The cascade overwhelmed all other sound, and perhaps its draft in that tight defile carried my scent downstream. Something moved within the rhododendron boughs that framed the top of the chute, and a bobcat stepped out of shadow onto the ledge. It glanced about as a housebound tabby might do upon entering a familiar room, then stepped across the thin sheet of water spread before the head of the plunge. It was gone as suddenly as it first appeared, but never knew it was seen, crossing the falls.

Another bobcat failed, I think, to sense us drift by in a canoe on a quiet stream. It stood with its front paws up against a tree bole and its tail erect, stretched out as if posing, looking over its shoulder away from our course. I pointed, and we both gawked until the current pushed us beyond. But it was there, and so were we. For all I know, that is how you see bobcats.

Blackberry; The Humblest Jewel

If you were tasked with designing a wild fruit to represent Western Pennsylvania, you might come up with the blackberry. Its familiar, arcing canes spread over logged hillsides and reclaimed strip mines, beside railroad tracks and across abandoned farmland reverting to woods. Blackberries are an unplanned bonus from hard-used land.

Such a luscious treat, blackberries lure us outdoors, and they're family-friendly; even small children can reach the fruit, which ripens in mid-summer when more elusive edibles like morels and ramps are gone. Their winey flavor and the satisfying grit of their inextricable seeds suit our tastes. But here, we like to earn our rewards, so even the blackberry's thorns fit our regional ethic.

We can even claim the world's flagship blackberry variety as our own. Blackberries are members of the Rose family (*Rosaceae*), which besides ornamental roses, also includes apples, peaches, and cherries. Some form of blackberry grows in most temperate parts of the world, with hundreds native to North America. Further subdivided, the blackberry belongs to the genus *Rubus*, one of the most complex and capricious groupings in all of botany. Some botanists recognize more than 700 blackberry species, pointing out minute differences in the shape of leaflet tips or the breadth of thorns at their base. Other scientists are less fastidious, clumping the 700 into 200 or even 30 species and writing off differences as variations within a type. Complicating blackberry classification, most species exhibit an easy willingness to hybridize, accepting diverse pollens left behind by bees to cross one subtly distinct type with another genetic outlier, presenting botanical organizers with another new challenge. Yet, amid that taxonomic morass, the most widely recognized blackberry of all is *Rubus allegheniensis*, the Allegheny blackberry, whose range across eastern North America bullseyes on Western Pennsylvania. Our Allegheny blackberry is so distinct and stable that it's also known as the "common blackberry" everywhere it grows.

That ebony nugget we call a blackberry is another enigma. It's not a berry at all. In botanical terms, it's an aggregate of drupelets, and if you know blackberries, if you've pricked your fingers to stain your tongue purple, you'll recall the cluster of tiny black globes attached to a white core. We think of the whole as a "berry," but each globe (drupelet) is an individual fruit with a seed inside. Think of a peach as an example. A peach is a botanical "drupe," a fleshy fruit surrounding a single central seed. Each of a blackberry's clumped globes is a small version of a peach. If peaches grew as an aggregate, like blackberries, the "berry" would be bigger than a basketball.

In a blackberry patch, the most robust canes are void of berries. Each cane takes two years to produce fruit. In its first season, the cane puts its energy into growth. Blossoms and berries appear in the second season after it has invested nutrients into reproduction, so the fruited cane appears drained and wan. But at any time, a blackberry patch will contain canes in both the growing and the fruit-bearing stage. Fruits develop from white rose-like blossoms that bloom in early summer.

No region has likely produced more gallons of homemade blackberry wine or more pints of blackberry jam than Western Pennsylvania. I like to go out in the morning in late July and early August when the air is still cool, when a song sparrow will sing from a crabapple nearby, and the glossy fruit is bejeweled with dew. But I don't mind the heat. Picking my way through a blackberry thicket, I like to feel the day warm as I gather mounds of black orbs, even the scent of which on my fingers conveys high summer in my part of the world.

Blackberries like full sun, so look for them in old fields and beside rural dirt roads. Sometimes, though, you will find the biggest, most luscious berries growing deep in a shaded thicket. Older people I knew as a boy called these "shade berries," and if the fruits were proclaimed "big as a thumb," you knew their picker had found a windfall whose location they were not likely to divulge.

If you find a good blackberry spot, make the most of it while you can. Prime blackberry thickets don't last long. Ecologists term the blackberry an "early successional" plant, evolved to exploit sunny locations in the aftermath of change. As the woods around the thicket stabilize and mature, blackberry patches phase out of existence. Making the most of a blackberry patch, though, doesn't mean tramping it into the ground. You'll see this too often, where prior pickers have all but destroyed a patch in their lust to get the ripe fruit quickly, paying no regard to those who might come after or to future seasons.

We're not alone in appreciating the blackberry. When snow lies deep and long, as it did last winter, cottontail rabbits gnaw the outer "bark" of blackberry canes. When the snow melts, you'll notice the rabbits' bright gnaw-marks high on the stem where a rabbit shouldn't be able to reach. As winter deepened, mounting snow lifted the cottontails ever higher to reach more blackberry bark when they needed it most. Bears and birds gorge on the fruit. Even box turtles seek out the fallen berries. Black bears can trample a patch almost as badly as human pickers, but bears are forgiven.

Picking blackberries requires no special equipment and no official sanction. There's nothing to buy, maintain, or license toward your enjoyment. A gallon milk jug is my primary vessel. I cut off the neck far enough down so that my hand fits into the top, but I keep the handle intact. My belt runs through the handle, so the jug hangs at my waist at the ideal height to receive berries, leaving both my hands free. When I fill the jug, I transfer that load to a 5-gallon bucket that's stashed nearby and start again.

You'll likely find yourself using one hand to hold and stabilize a cane while the other picks the berries. If you try to pluck berries from an unrestrained cane, the best will shake loose and fall, lost, into the leaf litter below. Fruit that dislodges easily favors dispersal of its seeds by birds and bears drawn to the sugar-laden lode. Mockingbirds, thrashers, waxwings, and other avian fruit-eaters can snatch a ripe berry with ease, then fly off to some similar spot to deposit the seeds. A bear can strip a dozen berries from a cane with one lick or by pulling the cane between its lips, heedless of thorns.

Later, the bear drops piles of gut-softened seeds in massive numbers, likely in another spot that favors germination as it forages elsewhere for berries.

When I pick blackberries, I always wear a sleeveless shirt. If you wear a long-sleeve shirt to protect your skin, the thorns will snag in the weave. Then, when you pull your arm free, the cane will recoil suddenly and dislodge the best fruit. Picking bare-armed, the thorns will drag across your skin, but they will not snag as they do in cloth, so you lose less fruit. You also tend to move your arms through the maze of canes with greater care when your arms are unprotected. Besides, I like to feel the sun on my skin. A network of scratches and a suntan add another element of satisfaction to a full bucket of berries.

I enjoy simple, repetitive tasks that require no technical or mechanical acumen. Picking blackberries on a summer day fits that formula. As your fruit bounty mounts, you sense a kind of rhythm taking over your movements, calming your thoughts. Pick, drop, survey, step ahead; These are simple actions that exploit the bond between human eye and human hand, with a tangible prize in the bargain. Something very old is at work, resurrected for a while in our attention-splintered lives. We are unaware of how we thirst for it until we feel it happen.

I pick berries now for pleasure and connection to place, for the succulent fruit and the pies it yields. But I remember men who picked blackberries out of need. In Fayette County, in the 1950s and '60s, blackberries grew in abundance among the ruins of coke ovens and along the railroad tracks that hauled coal from the mines. The best, most long-lived patch sprawled across a place we called the "pitholes," where coal shafts had subsided, leaving randomly scattered, cone-shaped craters, the breadth of an average motel room, across a hillside. Acrid smoke rose from some of the pits from underground fires, but blackberry thickets crawled throughout the craters. No trees could grow, so the canes basked there for years in a bonus of full sun.

When I was too young to gather berries myself, down-and-out men, some missing fingers or an arm, from work in the mines, would come to the door carrying water buckets brimming with blackberries they'd picked in the pitholes, offering them for sale for whatever my mother would give. I do not remember her ever turning them away.

Once, many years later, my son Aaron was eight or nine, and we were picking along a dirt road that skirts old fields in Ohiopyle State Park. We'd been at it all morning and were scratched, sunburned, and stained purple on the fingers and likely our lips. But we had a good haul of berries. An expensive sedan came crunching along the road, dust rising in its wake. The car slowed, then stopped, but we could not see the occupants through the tinted glass, which reflected blue sky and white clouds. The passenger window slid downward at a mechanically uniform speed, revealing the face of a young woman whose sunglasses reflected the same sky that had just disappeared with the window glass. The driver sat silent inside the car's deep gloom.

"What are you picking?" she asked.

Her question surprised us, and we hesitated.

"Blackberries."

"Those are poisonous, aren't they?" she queried.

"No, they're delicious," I said, stepping toward the car and extending a palmful of berries for her to sample.

Before I reached her, the window zoomed upward, reflecting again the glare of sky. Tires bit the gravel, and the car sped away, spearheading a cone of dust.

I still wonder about that encounter.

When I have filled my buckets after a session of picking, I indulge in a ritual I am willing to confide. I select a dozen or so of the best "specimen" blackberries within reach and cram them all in my mouth at once. Then I face the sun and bite down, smashing them into a mass of blackberry sensory overload—winey, pungent, warm, and tartly sweet. Then I know I have been out among the land at the height of summer, and there's not much I can do to know this better.

You can buy commercially grown blackberries in grocery stores now. They are large and uniform, nearly as large as "shade berries." But I think their buyers get a bad deal. No red-tail hawk screamed overhead at the produce counter, and no monotonous dry buzz of cicadas droned somewhere in the hazy distance. Store berries lack the waxy luster I see on wild fruits, and no heady fragrance lingers on still air. Store-bought berries to pile onto ice cream yield only a part of the reward of Rubus. The rest of it comes from being out there, piling them into a jug or a bucket, one by one.

Known to Crows

Once, some time ago, I heard crows cawing in the wooded hollow below my house. On impulse, I went inside and retrieved my crow call, which I've never used to hunt crows, but it has sometimes shocked sunrise gobbles from wild turkeys.

Crouching under boughs of the dense spruce that overhangs our back porch, I blew the call the way I learned from its printed instructions. Force a guttural cough up from your diaphragm and into the call, and a convincingly hoarse "Caw" grates out of the open tube. By the time I'd coughed a series of quick and urgent caws, the air above those woods boiled with black birds.

They rose above the treetops in pairs, trios, and fours, then assembled as a wheeling swarm over the house. Their cries stabbed down shrill and angry, "Caw! Caw! Caw!" as insults laden with petulant scorn. The swirl drew yet more crows from afar, streaking in as singles and pairs, dark arrows from the north, northeast, and behind me from the south. Each newcomer hurled its own shrieks into the din, diving into the tempest as if that vortex of opaque shapes had spawned its own gravity at its hub.

Some crows dove low, peering into my sheltering spruce from glossed and menacing eyes, then raked the air hard to clear the roof. Profoundly entertained, I wondered: "What did I say?"

As an experiment, I stepped into the open, and the funnel-cloud of birds hushed, disassembled, and melted into the trees like vapors on a gust of wind.

Though I've tried many times, I have never been able to incite such a crow-riot again. Now, when I hear crows in the woods and cough through the call, there's a silence. Any crows within earshot lift off their perches, caw briefly in a different, more languid tenor and drift away over the hills, their indifferent calls receding.

Their repeated snubs prompted more deliberate reading about crows. They and their *Corvidae* allies, ravens and magpies, are among the most intelligent animals on earth, rivaling primates in various kinds of cognition. Researchers believe—all but know, really—that crows can count, and careful experiments prove they can recognize individual human faces, link them with past events, and communicate that association to other crows. Behavioral scientists call that skill "temporal and spatial displacement," once presumed to be an exclusively human trait.

I believe I've seen this cleverness applied. The crows I once lured and provoked know where I live, and they've warned other younger crows to ignore my mimicry. Paying attention to nature, you don't have to go far from home to be astonished.

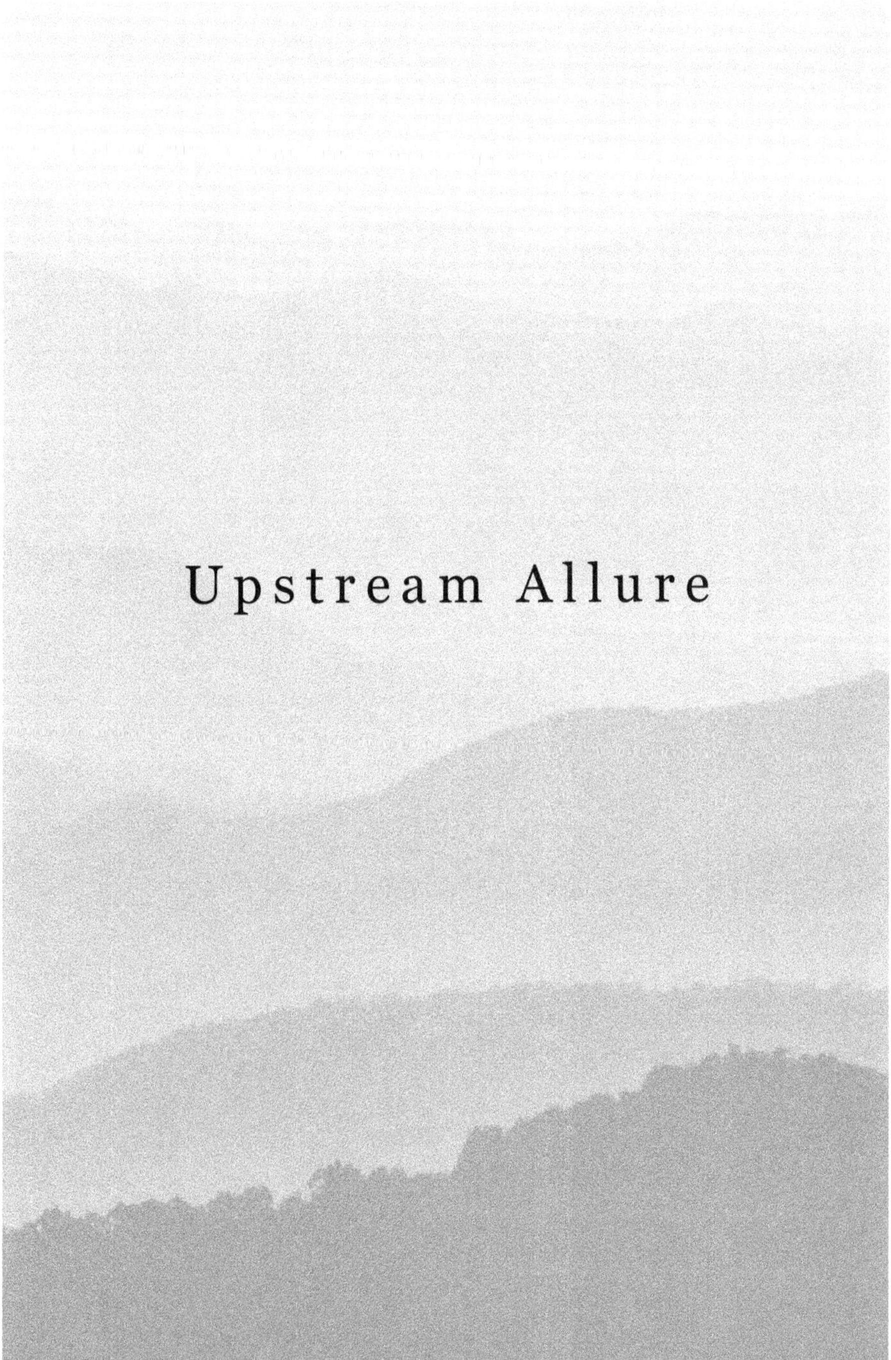

Upstream Allure

At the Heart of Hollows

To my thinking, "Appalachian" is a positive modifier. Forested hollows embrace you here, draw you inward and up along chattering creeks. Misty knobs stand as touchstones of potential when routine keeps you out of the woods. Many of the people rooted here are inspirations, and no region displays the polarity of its seasons with such abandon as Appalachia. Trout live here too, furtive and lurking in the land's wrinkled innards, like a bonus prize concealed inside an already ostentatious gift.

I feel a debt to trout, best expressed through a question. If it weren't for trout and their allure, would I know these mountains as I do? Would I have exchanged so much of their cool, rich atmosphere through my lungs? More pragmatically, would I care what happens to this land, its water, what it offers my children, had I not stalked these creeks in a quest for small fish—even one trout per outing, for numbers don't mean much in fishing. It's the moment of contact that counts, that blurring of boundary between self and all else, which can happen with one trout as well as 20, perhaps more so.

Mississippi-bound creeks in western Pennsylvania and West Virginia host most of my fishing. Streams I fish flow among others that present a tragic regional paradox. Appalachia's western slope—the Allegheny Range—harbors one of the densest braids of stream-miles on the planet. Trout fishing, then, "should be" limitless. But the region also experienced two distinct coal eras. The first lasted a hundred million years as fern forests fell, entombed in the swamps that birthed them. The Appalachian uplift and a half-billion subsequent years compressed that muck into coal. The second coal age was much shorter, more recent, but equally transformative. From 1900 to 1980 or so (to the present in some places), reckless mining defiled the headwaters, gnawing at the contours like a caterpillar chewing its way along a leaf-margin, venting acid, aluminum, and iron downstream so that people grew up believing streams here were meant to flow orange, and that trout, if they imagined them, were for other places. I assumed so myself until I probed the surviving hollows.

Coal is still mined here but the pace is slacking, and people are less resigned now to ruin. Even more uplifting, the tenacious hard work of local watershed groups and Trout Unlimited chapters is restoring streams across the region to life. To lift a trout from pristine water that has never suffered the degradation of heedless resource extraction within its watershed is a kind of joy every angler should know in their fishing career. To fish a stream that's been rescued from such violation by the noble work of people you know personally, people who have resolved that a stream void of life in their home region, on their watch, is beyond toleration, is to know angling satisfaction at a supreme degree. A trout lifted from such water has another aspect to it. It embodies not the easy sound-bite-slogan progress of stripping and drilling but the hard, genuine progress of natural resource restoration. Such a fish is a symbol for hope, an incentive to strive.

This spring, in early May, I fished all day in the rain, rather in intermittent pulses of rain. Drizzle oozed out of overcast chill, gathering into bouts of downpour. Each deluge ushered an encore of sun, when mist rose and filtered, then the cycle repeated. The stream swelled and ebbed, clouded and cleared around me. No hatch was apparent amid the flux, and no trout rose. So, I resorted to default and cast a cone-head black woolly bugger to likely places. Some look askance at this ungainly big fly, but I like its versatility when the fish divulge no clues. I dead-drifted it through seams, watching the line for a pickup. I swung it downstream, then stripped it back up, cast up and stripped it down. Well into the day, I noticed that something about the rhythm of that way of fishing supplanted fatigue, and I felt energized, a reminder of younger adventures. I decided to go with it long as it lasted, and I kept casting, stripping, moving upstream.

Somewhere along that ascent, I took a breath, and the perfume of mountain azalea was on the air, sweet and languid. At times the scent was strong, then fleeting, like bits of a dream you can't reconstruct. Upstream, an azalea was blooming, its fragrance carried along by the drag of the current. If you have never scented wild azalea, originating from somewhere unseen on a damp, cool day in the Allegheny Mountains, it is worth the trip from where you are reading this. It's like trading ordinary breath for some poignant vestige of memory—of a girl maybe, from long ago, of romance missed and regretted through dearth of courage.

I am not skilled with bird song, but as I fished upward into the strengthening azalea spoor, I could nail the nearby songs of hooded and black-throated blue warblers, one of the vireo clan, and the melodic trill of a wood thrush, which is the auditory equal to wild azalea's scent. It was already a rewarding day when something astonishing happened. On this stream, I am satisfied—elated, actually—with small to moderate-size trout. Yet, within 20 minutes of one another, during one of those spans when the water was clearing, I caught the two largest brown trout that have come to my hand in 35 years of fishing that creek. Both hit the bugger in fast water on a downstream strip, and both made the reel squeal, yielding line.

If, as I believe, we fish to be immersed in a place, to sense its inherent, ambient heart, and are buoyed by that union, and then if beyond such attainment, we also feel the outright thrill of catching exceptional specimens of the quarry that lured us there, what success can surpass that in angling? I'm at a loss to imagine it.

Yet, something was missing that day, something that, by its absence, felt obtrusive. I knew what it was without deliberate consideration, and I might have traded the brief rush of landing those two big browns for the familiar boost of hearing a ruffed grouse drum, as I am so accustomed there. But the northern advance of West Nile virus, aided by warmer climate, has hit grouse hard, and you must climb out of the creek hollows to the high ridges to find one. Here, where I followed my dad, uncles and their English setters on grouse hunts as a boy who could barely keep up, grouse leave an inescapable void.

Another morning, not long ago, I fished farther downstream on the same creek below a cascade framed in hemlock that could be a *Scenic*

America calendar cover, but I'm glad is not. Anonymity these days is a declining resource.

Despite the waterfall's comfortable din, I could hear an unrecognized warbler song. The bird was singing nearby, concealed in foliage, somewhere above the spot where a trout was rising to a rhythm of its own. My hope of identifying the singer distracted my concentration from the trout. The bird would sing, and I'd peer for it. Then the trout would rise, and I'd try to discern its insect of interest. This conflicting enterprise was something like watching a vertically oriented ping-pong match. I never learned what bug the fish was gulping, but finally, I ignored the warbler long enough to drop a No. 16 Light Cahill on the bulge just above the trout's station. The fly did one pirouette from leader tension, and the trout rose and slurped, one of those affirming takes of implicit trust that inflates your angler's self-image—until the next time. Hiking back out to the truck, I wondered which of the two outcomes would have been more rewarding—enticing the trout or getting to know a new warbler call. I don't have the answer, but I'm fortunate to face such appealing quandaries along these rugged ravines I fish.

A smaller run vents itself directly into a brawling river deep in a gorge. Only brook trout live there, native salmonid gems, marooned in their steep basin. It takes a hike to fish there, plus a taxing uphill return, and I carry a sandwich or two in my pack.

I'd fished upstream to an inviting ledge of sandstone in the sun, which doesn't strike into that canyon for long. Nearby, impossible to miss, shone the bright green, paired and upright leaves of a big patch of "ramps" (*Allium tricoccum*). This potent botanical kin to leeks and garlic is an Appalachian icon. Mountain people sought them for generations in early spring, craving fresh greens after a winter diet of dried beans and salted meat. Nowadays, urbane restaurants in big cities proffer ramps as haute cuisine. I prefer to dig my own ramps, and most trout streams here lead me to them. I don't consider it spring until I've "tainted" my breath with their redolence.

I leaned the rod into laurel, pulled a pocketknife and dug out a dozen. Ramps are a lot like the "old-timer" mountain people I recall from childhood, so embedded in soil and rock that they are hard to uproot. I washed my ramps in the creek until the bulbs were creamy white, appetizing, and pared off the rootlets. Then I lifted the top slice of bread on a sandwich and aligned them, green leaves and all, atop ham.

After lunch, I stretched out on the sun-warmed shelf with my pack for a pillow and plummeted into that kind of sleep born of satisfied exertion in comforting surroundings.

Some odd snuffling sound woke me, disquietingly near. I rose on an elbow and looked into the eyes of two black bears, their snouts flecked with humus. They'd been rooting for ramps in the same patch where I gleaned my garnish, and their breath, no doubt, was equally enriched. Both bears sprinted up the slope, pausing once to look back. Fully awake, I resumed fishing, pleased that my menu choice was endorsed by the locals.

The most natively inviting place I know is the headwater basin of a trout stream, where I try to fish a couple of times every spring. I "try" because there are no quick evening visits there, no impromptu stops on the way to somewhere else. To fish these headwaters in the way they deserve, you must reserve and invest a day. The hike upstream, the fords across lesser sections to keep to the trail, and finally, the deliberate probing of every sublime spot in a necklace of plunges and pools require that time. This is a place where you dare not hurry because there is too much to miss. If I sense myself doing so, from some inner roil, I stop, head back downstream, and fish near the road.

Hiking upstream, everywhere you look is native beauty, not one thing that doesn't belong, and the eye knows that somehow. No vulgar advance of alien garlic mustard yet supplants shy wildflowers, and no rank march of multi-flora rose smothers the thickets. Once, I did spot a pioneering stalk of Japanese knotweed thrusting up from a silt bar. I tore it out as deep as I could and stuffed it down my waders so no shred of it could possibly propagate, then covered the spot with the biggest flat rock I could carry, to smother its roots.

To fish there on a May morning is to know what the native heart of Appalachia is supposed to be like. The roots of big hemlocks embrace grainy sandstone boulders at streamside, and massive beeches, their smooth gray bark clawed by bears, arch over the flow. Moss drapes logs and rocks, soaking in rainfall so that it impounds inside a living sponge, then drips slow, steady and cold to collect as a creek. The cool moistness of the place feels right, and the subdued quality of light ignites pale blooms of trillium, violet, and bellwort across the slopes.

Once, I saw a bald eagle there, which challenged my notions about the big raptor's habitat. I'd only seen eagles on coastal salt marsh, on North-woods canoe country lakes, or over broad rivers like the Allegheny, where they can soar and scan for fish. But that morning, I snuck up to a pool on this little creek, so intent on trout that I ignored all surroundings. A blurred motion above me attracted my glance, and I looked up at an adult bald eagle launching off a snag that jutted over the flow. The bird bored straight downstream, hemmed in by woods. It would need to veer and careen at low altitude for a long way before the canopy opened, releasing it to a broader sky. Relieved of its fierce burden, that snag-perch whipped up and down for a long time after the eagle banked around the first downstream curve, gone from my sight.

I have been hiking up there to fish ever since one long-ago opening day of trout season when my father led my sister and me upstream to escape the crowds. We snuck low through the laurel, watchful for timber rattlers, and dangled Mickey Finn streamers at the heads of pools. The little wild brook trout always struck on the first cast into a hole, and when you slid one across your palm—firm, smooth, and speckled—your breath caught in your throat at the miracle of it. It felt like we were privileged to know some sweet secret the hills concealed.

One evening not so long ago, but when there were still grouse in the hollows, I fished upstream to a cock ruff's intermittent tattoo. It's an odd sound that you feel as much as hear, an accelerating thump inside your own ribcage that fools you at first as if it were your own errant heartbeat.

A modest hatch of drakes lumbered through the gloom, and I stalked upstream, making short casts to every pool, torn between the pleasure of catching trout and knowing it would be dark when I got back to the truck.

The grouse drummed as I admired one of those little char for a moment before its release. Just as the rolling concussion climaxed, a whitetail doe stepped across the stream above. It struck me in that moment when I held the trout, heard a grouse and watched that deer, that I hunkered under ancient hemlocks, and that mounds of blooming mountain laurel, their flower clusters big as softballs and hot-pink in the gloom, enflamed the ravine. I realized that I'd beheld, in one way or another, each of my home state of Pennsylvania's official symbols—its state bird, fish, mammal, tree, and flower—in one place at the same time. I wondered how many people have been privileged to encounter these all at once, as I did, or had noted it if they had. I knew in the same moment that, for me, fishing made such a fortunate juxtaposition accessible.

The designation of such symbols appeals to me. It represents one of society's few official nods to the worth of wild things and conveys the crucial truth that wonder in nature needs not the exotic; indeed, that wonder can be, should be, inspired by the native and near.

Last fall, relatives invited me along, at a discount, on a trip to the Galapagos Islands, the planet's acknowledged showcase of ecological concepts. It was a tempting opportunity, and I'd like to go someday. But this excursion was to be in spring, when bloodroot blooms in the Earth's most ancient mountains and when birds of such lovely plumage that most people would assign them to TV nature shows are filtering, largely unnoticed, through Appalachia's hardwood canopy. It's one thing to be ferried around with other tourists and be shown wonders by a guide. It's quite another to renew acquaintance, on personal terms, with miracles which, though familiar, never fail to awe. One never knows how many more springs one can count on.

Summer's Upstream Allure

It's difficult to say what prompts a late-summer trout sortie. Prime fishing over hatches and rises tapered off with the long-gone solstice. Flows are slack, no tugging at wader folds. Trout brood in the shade of ledges, more likely to show you their wakes, flushed like grouse from cover than to slick your palm. Still, that rod case in the corner snags your eye every time you leave the house. The neglect of it feels amiss. How many more fishing seasons do you have, prime time or not? For certain, it's fewer than you've breezed through, paying too little attention. So, you go.

This time you go with a good friend, one you know doesn't need to catch fish as sharply as he needs to be along the water of wild hollows. That knowledge is a good beginning. It smooths out every other unknown in the day ahead. That first step upstream makes a success. From there, it's gravy.

Fishing a little mountain creek with such a friend in late summer is courtesy incarnate, choreographed as leap-frog. You fish one hole; he fishes the next. You loop around one another with exaggerated stealth because that's important—to the fishing and to the respect you harbor for the other's experience and space. If he hooks a fish during this dance, it's as good—it's the same—as if you had done so yourself. There's mystery in that, but you don't dwell on it. It's one of those things better sensed than understood.

Leap-frog works until the hollow tightens, its outcrops and ledges with their white-knuckling hemlock roots demanding a steep climb on slick soles, then a scary descent to get back to the stream ahead. So, from there, you follow one another, trying not to be one more among the numberless obstacles to back-cast, taking turns.

The air is dense there in sheltered woods. It's "air you can wear," as one friend quips of the mugginess that wets without wading. Sounds are primal, easy to sort. The creek's murmur is the base, always there, so that after you've fished seven hours within it, you carry it home in your head like a stuck song but better because nobody wrote it. Harmony to creek song is the relentless whine of mosquitoes, close at your ear, insistent. Somehow, their hordes don't seem a nuisance. They're just part of what you accepted when you stepped upstream. Squeals of jays and hawk-shrieks are accents.

To fish with as much confidence as can be had there, hang tiny nymphs beneath bushy dry flies—caddis or stimulators—on short 7X droppers. You can get good drifts with that rig through the bucket-size runs where a brookie might lurk. On most takes, the dry fly, as indicator of what's happening below, will dive, but sometimes a trout eats the indicator itself. That's gravy too.

But to fish that setup, you've got to rig it, and knotting 7X mono around the open bend of a dry fly hook is getting to be a test. Holding it so it's backlit by black clothing or the darkest rock you can find helps you see it. Then, its fine suppleness resists your over-taxed fingertips' strain to coax the tag end through its target loop. Just as you get that tag threaded, its end snags on your own fingerprint whorl, as if that tiny channel were some immovable buttress, yet it's your own offending flesh. Finally, at the moment to tighten, a mosquito whines into your ear and stabs. If you lose this knot, you'll have to re-tie or quit fishing. Your capability is that taxed. Do you knot or swat?

If you are fortunate, you will catch trout. If you are supremely fortunate, those trout will be wild brook trout, the resilient char of these green mountains of unknowable age. An angler, you will wish them to be large fish, but they won't be. They will fit across your palm, which is perfectly fine and right because you can behold them well there, which is a privilege known to few, and because you know they are doing their best here, where rich food is scarce and dangers many. If everything good and right about these hollows could be distilled into one tiny point, that rightness would be inside this fish. Its brief sequester in your hand is a gift of this place and your effort.

You think about the hefty mess of sunfish you caught last week, kept for fillets and delicious. They were fine fish, colored-up males mostly, but they meant less in the context of your life than this one brook trout in hand. They can live in lots of places, man-made ponds and natural backwaters. This trout can only be here, under these folded ridges, luring you upstream yet again.

The Thrill of Near Distance

A fishing trip's allure can be more about mind than miles. I know this because our immediate family did not travel to fish. My dad ran a small business, the demands of which grew most acute as trout season opened in April, then pressed unrelentingly through fall. We fished when he could, close to home. So sequestered, toting flyrods to exotic locales was not a quest we much envisioned.

Our nearest stream was Dunbar Creek, endowed by history with an inglorious air. It had been named for Thomas Dunbar, a tremulous colonel in General Braddock's disastrous march across the Alleghenies to expel the French from British claims in 1755. When the French and their Indian allies routed Braddock on the Monongahela River, Dunbar might have made a difference by counterattack. Instead, he held his assigned ground far to the rear, then dumped all supplies and skedaddled fast over the mountains to Philadelphia. Dunbar Creek's tainted repute deepened in my childhood when headwater strip mines bled acid downstream so that when my dad and I fished evenings or Sundays, its marginal conditions supported only trout stocked in recent days by the state.

Even then, the Pennsylvania Fish Commission designated Dunbar Creek for fly-fishing-only. The rule did lighten fishing pressure, and I credit living near a stream so constrained for my becoming a fly-angler, but it was an odd place to learn. Dunbar's mine-acid infusion harbored no bugs, so with no hatches to match, we learned little of aquatic entomology. Our go-to flies were a Black Ghost streamer and a simple contrivance we called the "honey bug," tan chenille wrapped robustly around a hook-shank, without hackle, resembling nothing so much as a hatchery feed-pellet.

My Uncle Max, younger brother to my mother, was the angler-explorer among my kin. On his days off from delivering for United Parcel, he roved north to more pristine reaches of the Allegheny Plateau and south to West Virginia's wild Potomac highlands, prospecting for better fishing. Sometime in the mid-1960s, he found his way to the Cranberry River, a tannin-stained and lightly-fished gem that flowed beneath red spruce-clad peaks of the Monongahela National Forest. Trout fishing on the 'Berry, as Uncle Max abbreviated the name to flaunt familiarity, was like nothing we home-bounds could imagine. But soon after his discovery, he invited me along to fish the 'Berry with him and his son, my cousin, Doug. I was entering adolescence. Doug was eight or nine.

The Cranberry River was one state border, one hundred-some miles, and four hours south from home over West Virginia's 1960s road network. But it could have been an Alaskan char and rainbow lode for the excitement it stoked. That Alaskan link strengthened when we drew near, crammed among tackle and gear in Uncle Max's Falcon station wagon, and stopped at the trailhead for the Cranberry Glades. From a rickety boardwalk, "the Glades" still spread out flat and boggy, probing treeless tentacles between surrounding knobs, startlingly out of place in a craggy forest ocean. But "out of place" is a forgivable impression. The Glades are a spongey relict of arctic tundra left atop the Alleghenies when the last ice age waned, where red-tea rivulets course among pitcher plants, wild cranberry, and sundews, spill westward, then assemble as the Cranberry River—"river" being generously applied to modest streams tumbling off West Virginia's high backbone.

Uncle Max's explanation for the Cranberry's fine fishing was that it was not easy to reach, even after the serpentine drive through places with quizzical names like Junior, Mingo, and Slatyfork. You couldn't get to the fishing by vehicle like we did back home, where other locals drove into Dunbar Creek at shallow fords to wash their cars. Our last leg to the 'Berry was a dirt-and-gravel U. S. Forest Service track that courted the river through the national forest, 16 miles in all, forming the administrative boundary between the Cranberry Wilderness to its north and the Cranberry

Backcountry southward. But that rutted lane was gated and locked at the top, enabling the West Virginia DNR to stock the river where, otherwise, the Forest Service permitted no motorized travel.

Spurred by my uncle's prior success, our goal was a campsite at the mouth of Houselog Run, a 'Berry tributary eight miles from the car. We had prepped for weeks to get there by bicycle—not the sleek backcountry bikes of today, but conventional kids' bikes for which Uncle Max had cleverly rigged a plywood deck resting on the back fender and bolted to the rear axle by aluminum struts. Atop those foot-and-a-half-wide boards, we piled tent, sleeping bags, Coleman stove, food, and rod cases, then strapped it all down with rubber thongs cut from a truck-tire innertube. The '60s were sunset to the era when much outdoor gear was still improvised, a source of pride for innovators. But mounted up, we looked like beetles on bikes—handlebar antennae, a rider-thorax, with abdomen bulging behind.

Jouncing over bedrock and gravel against straining brakes, we hit the river at three miles in, where the track relaxed to moderate grade. From there, we flanked the Cranberry downstream, gawking at Yew Mountain towering to the south and pods of trout in clear pools. Doug and I chafed to break out the rods, but Uncle Max advised we make camp before fishing.

Halfway to Houselog, he called a halt at a place that became a ritual rest stop on all my subsequent trips, solo or with companions, where tiny but reliable Lost Run chattered over a cliff within a bike-rider's reach. From the first time I was present in that spot, it exuded some sacred sense. This was in June, and the air was cooler there, dragged by the run from high hollows and laden with something alive—spruce forest? Arctic fen? A tobacco-brown Forest Service sign with routed yellow letters proclaimed "Lost Run" in the middle of nowhere, affirming its strangely secular holiness. We leaned the bikes into rock-cliff and slurped cupped handfuls so cold your eyes ached while your throat soaked in pleasure, and the mineral tang of a mountain's innards spiced your tongue.

Reaching the river was quicker on bicycles than other methods employed by the few anglers we encountered—horseback or on foot with backpacks. But getting back out with a bike was the toughest option on a coarse road too steep to pedal, where you had to push that awkward conveyance uphill. Our obsession had been getting there to fish. All else was afterthought, even the reciprocal toil we'd made for ourselves by a down-mountain careen.

Relief always attends reaching a campsite after rough travel, especially one of backcountry comfort. Our Houselog camp was south of the road, officially in the "backcountry," where camping rules are less rigid than in wilderness, a fly-cast to the north. A perennial fire-ring beckoned, with cast-off refrigerator-rack grill and encircling seats of log and rock. There was a frame of beech branches lashed to trees to support a tarp for meals in the rain, and some soul had left a mound of firewood covered by plastic sheeting. Uncle Max told us that was the mark of an upstanding camper, to leave dry wood for the next anonymous occupant. His remark bore the impact of simple, decent sense. We set up our tent, hung the tarp and lantern, arrayed our cooking gear and, then, rigged our rods. It was time to fish the 'Berry.

Even that long June evening was waning when we parked the bikes another mile downriver at a long pool you could scan from the trail. No other person was in sight, but trout were rising across a hundred-yard span of river, shouldering up molten ripples that rolled and collided in the dying light. Before that twilight session, I'd never caught a trout on a dry fly, and am not certain I'd ever seen one feed at the surface. I had no idea what the fish were gulping, but I'd read that the Adams was a universal imitator and had tied some acceptable specimens for the trip.

No clinch knot I have ever tied was forged with shakier fingers. After weeks of imagined hookups, an up-and-down car ride through hairpin turns on mountain roads, and a lurching descent by bike, my hand-fashioned Adams was ready to float over trout. I clambered over boulders while Doug and his dad watched, took a stance, and cast. The fly was still pivoting from leader tension when a trout engulfed it. I struck, felt that sensuous writhe, then nothing. My knot had pulled, and my fly was gone, leaving its spoor of pig-tailed tippet.

In deepening gloom, atmospheric and emotional, I was desperate to catch a fish but could command neither fingers nor concentration. I lost three more Adams to slurping trout and failed knots before it grew too dark to bind another, and we pedaled back, me in a funk. We gathered at the fire and made plans to fish that same pool after breakfast, beginning one of the longest outdoor nights of my life.

The pool was tranquil on our return, but with the whole day ahead and more composed, I secured and cast an Adams. It was ignored. Uncle Max instructed on line-mending, but the trout were apathetic. Just downstream, Doug flipped lures with his spin-cast rig, landing fish and whooping to his approving father. The hardware route tempted, and a spare spin outfit leaned against the beech frame in camp, but that morning seemed the time and place to cement a fly-fishing perception of self. I persisted.

All fly-tiers will recall this little indulgence from early endeavors. You labor at the vise crafting somber patterns that, while known to be effective, get tedious to tie. You crave eye candy. Color plates in a book I'd borrowed showed ranks of riotous-hued variety. One pattern snagged my eye as compromise between garish and grave—the Orange Fish Hawk—a wet fly whose lurid orange body, ribbed in silver tinsel, was redeemed by a cloak of grizzly hackle. Smitten, I'd tied many.

With one split-shot leading the way, I lobbed a fish hawk into the darkest, tea-stained seam I could reach. The line settled and twitched, and I lifted the rod against that miraculous throb so intensely received in eager adolescence. The fish was a sleek rainbow, and many more like it slashed those orange-and-grizzly hawks, drawn, as I had been, to the dual visage of flash and reserve. Nearby, in cool stillness before the sun struck the depths of the gorge, Doug and Uncle Max played their own eager fish. As a trio alone, we shared that kind of morning some entitled seed within yourself assumes will come to you frequent and routine throughout your fishing life, while another, more fatal muse whispers to note it all and remember because there will not be many to equal it.

We did not think about catch-and-release back then, except when we'd approached the limit of six, cull-releasing smaller trout in hope of a big one. But taking fish home, packed in the duffle for the push up the mountain, was in no way practical. On the Cranberry, we killed stocked trout for the suppers in camp.

We always went a short distance up some tributary to gut our trout, where, before you had finished, crayfish scuttled from under rocks to drag away pink offal. At fireside, we rolled the fish in flour and pepper, then placed them, sputtering, into seething grease saved from the bacon we'd used up first, then stored its translucent fat, hung in our bear bag, for frying trout throughout the trip. We did the fish on the Coleman because its flame was consistent. You had to turn them with two hands, one wielding the worn spatula, the other a fork to ease the fish back into the popping hot grease. No one ever minded doing the cooking. It placed you at the center of satisfied revel, and you caught the aroma at its most potent—the river's clean essence, melded with smoke, fat, and salt.

Another skillet of fried potatoes browned on the campfire grill, and we didn't much care if they scorched. We mounded the spuds, steaming, on aluminum plates, capped by a tier of bronzed trout, fins and tail crisped, draped across the summit. Then we'd settle back and grin at one another through the flames.

I learned that if you inserted a fork in the lateral line, you could slide the succulent meat free by pulling "with the grain" away from the mid-line in the direction the bones were arrayed. You could work your way down the body, alternating mouthfuls of mealy potatoes, then peel out the supple skeleton, intact, held up in celebratory display to your dining companions. Flipped into the fire, the skeleton curled and glowed, and you could eat the plate-side fillet without caution.

Such a meal cannot be mimicked in tamer settings. It is communion with companions and the surroundings from which you gleaned it. The imperative of catch-and-release in modern fishing is acknowledged and respected, but there was something about those fish feasts on the Cranberry that closed an essential circle, propelling those present toward trout in rugged places for life.

Some years, our Cranberry trips fell in April when you could season your trout and potatoes with fried "ramps," reeking wild kin to leeks, and icons of Appalachian culture. I'd heard old people at home speak of ramps but had never there found a place where they grew. Ramps did thrust up their twin leaves in April, in sheltered hollows where Cranberry feeder-streams stair-stepped toward the river and phoebes flushed out from their nests beneath dripping ledges. We'd venture up past the waterfalls and dig a few handfuls from rocky humus with a pocketknife, then wash the creamy-white bulbs in the creek to zest that night's supper and mark our breath for days.

On ramp forays, I'd carry my flyrod, halved and cased. Brook trout, wild there, graced every one of those cold and shaded feeder creeks— Houselog, Tumbling Rock, and Birchlog runs. If you fished with stealth, they streaked out from under rock or root for any fly you offered, then fought with courage that belied their size. We never killed the natives. We caught them to behold them. Marooned on your palm, they looked like dense bars of acrylic shimmer, azure-speckled and olive-parred, so elegant you could not avoid a long moment's gape before tilting your hand so the fish would slip back, then dart into shadow. Later, approaching sleep, you envisioned those small char nosed in under some intimate cascade, veiled in hoary tumbling lather lit by the moon. You knew they were there, and the trip home was fuller for knowing.

Those fish were opposites in every way to another variety of trout that, admittedly, spiked our Cranberry adventures with glamor—the West Virginia Centennial golden trout, not to be confused with the true golden trout of California's High Sierra. West Virginia hatchery staff nurtured this golden trout into being in the 1950s from one ancestral rainbow with mutant gold spots. By 1963, its descendants were gilded all over, and the state had enough to stock across the mountains in celebration of West Virginia's birth at the height of the Civil War, when Virginia's western counties forsook the Old Dominion and rejoined the Union as a sovereign free state. Anglers went feverish for them, and Doug and I were in no way immune. You couldn't help it. Even in the 'Berry's tea-tint, their garishness jumped out at the eye like neon to an inebriate on a foggy night.

Doug and I spied a big golden once on a down-river scout while Uncle Max relaxed in camp. It was holed up in a dark root-crater pried out when a hemlock toppled between the river and the road. We dropped the bikes and spent hours trying to catch it.

These novelty rainbows are known for a mercurial schizophrenia, acquired perhaps as chromosomal coincidence of gold pigment. It's hard to predict what one will hit, and they're spooky, given to random meanders for no apparent cause. This one ignored every fly I presented, even the orange fish hawks. Doug resorted to salmon eggs, often a golden trout's Achilles heel, but our quarry showed no interest. More oddly, it held its position despite our encroachments, finning in the current with fluid grace.

We needed to resolve that standoff, so I suggested that Doug poke the fish with the tip of his stubby spin-cast rod just to see it abandon its station. He did, but the thing snubbed his torment, not even sidling away in avoidance. Such complacence was baffling. Maybe it was hurt, I opined to Doug and reached deep with a hand to touch the fish.

We were not accustomed to litter along the Cranberry and did not expect its mar. Few anglers made the effort to get there, effort that filtered out boorish litterbugs by default. When I stretched an arm into the river's chill, I felt not a fish's firm side but pliant film. I clutched at its weightlessness and lifted out a bright yellow bread bag that had snagged on a root after some lout discarded it upstream. Doug and I stared at one another, our gullibility dawning, then scanned the stream for witnesses. There were none, save this account. But that yellow plastic was the first evidence that the Cranberry River was not as far from home as it had seemed to two cousins.

I have since toted a flyrod to vaunted locales—Idaho, Montana, Alaska—pursuing other bright fish. But no journey after those first 'Berry trips took me farther beyond my point of reference in fishing. They granted the encouragement of early achievement and revealed Appalachia's unsullied heart, upon whose fringe I had drawn every breath of my life but had never known or beheld. I took my son to the 'Berry many years afterward. It was the right thing to do.

Blood and Tea

Smoke To See By

Greasy smoke from a reluctant fire smarts in my eyes and probes my nose. I'm accustomed to the sting, and I don't recoil. Brief discomfort is a fair trade for the swell of warmth and the spicy whiff of hickory behind the smoke's acrid assault. Still, a smear of tears wells up in my squint, distorting the snowflakes into gauzy streaks against the dark water beyond. Somehow, the distortion ushers a clarity in which I see the worth of the wooded hills around me and my good fortune to have known them and shared them.

I am fireside at my spare campsite on a lake in a wooded hollow. It is the last day of deer season, and a sleek doe hangs head-down from the meat pole I erected beside the water. The deer looks as if it had hardly suffered trauma. Shot well and kept carefully uphill from the blood in the field dressing, then dragged the short distance downhill over thin fresh snow. The sleek glossy pelt is clean and lies true to its grain, and the plume of white tail curves outward and down, a mirror image of its position in living flight.

Like countless others, the hollow that harbors this lake backs up into the western fringe of the Allegheny Plateau, a wrinkled sprawl of hills that ramble and roll westward across the Ohio River to ease into prairie lands. It is not what qualifies as spectacular country, but it is good country. Wild things and experiences linked to them are accessible here, near at hand. That which was spectacular here no living person has known—native forest with oak as broad as a bass boat, white pine worthy of ships' masts, hemlock and holly mingled along the streams. But a new forest is back now, reclaiming pastures and strip mines with a younger, scruffier growth that is the best we can have for now, and we'll take it.

This lake is really a pond, I suppose, but I like to think of it as a lake because of the sound of it in my own head. The terms "lake" and "pond" deal with definitional nuance, of course, but lake or pond, this impoundment has been the host of many encounters, at the center of many insights. In justification, it is not round as ponds tend to be in this part of the world, gouged into some flat spot behind a barn. This pond is long and narrow, backing up from an earthen clay dam—overgrown now and barely discernible—into its natal hollow between steep slopes of poplar woods, far enough so that paddling a canoe up toward the tapering end, shrouded in cattail where wood ducks loaf, holds a sense of small adventure. The up-lake shallows are distant enough from my campsite so that backing a camouflaged kayak into the cattails before dawn, over a yielding skim of ice to await those ducks feels plausible. In early summer, broad, flame-breasted bluegills fin over spawning redds in the poplar shade. A dry fly cast from the same craft will just have time to right itself on the surface film before disappearing in an exuberant swirl, its assailant tugging with torque and heart enough to pivot the boat like a bumped compass's needle returning to north. In the shallows, the bluegills are safe from the cormorant I once saw paddling and diving on the lake, 400 miles from its coastal haunts. It stayed always at the lake's exact midpoint as if it shunned these enclosing hills. The fish are not safe, though, from the herons. Green herons and great blues stand in the algae with the stillness of snakes, watchful, certain.

Nor are the bluegills safe from the lake's big snapping turtles except, perhaps, as individuals within the protective security of their own vast numbers, which makes the capture of any one fish unlikely. I watched a snapper once, hunting bluegills along the bottom at night. It was as heedless of my flashlight's beam as it seemed of time itself. Without stirring the fine silt, it bottom-walked toward a pod of bluegills then stopped a foot away. From there, it oozed toward the oblivious fish with no perceptible movements of its limbs, the way spilled coffee seeps through paper towels. Then it paused as if coiling some inner spring, and its jaws shot forward with such alien quickness that I was aware only of a slight stirring of silt and some odd suggestion of sound that had somehow accomplished the sonic transcendence from water to air. After the flash of movement, there in my LED beam, two inches of fish tail stuck out from one side of a chisel-shaped head at the end of an outstretched saurian neck. The last I saw of the encounter were the pale undersides of broad, clawed feet as the turtle paddled down into darkness.

Predators of all kinds are everywhere here around my camp. It feels more right, though, to think of them as "hunters." The term "predator" carries judgment within it, implying a taking from "us," from we rightful human executors, who should have first options on all takings. Though this place once produced mutton and beef, buckwheat and corn, it's now more food chain than a farm. Here, where I twice have found the splayed remains of a deer among eager coyote tracks on the blood-stained lake ice, where a hawk once struck a grouse I was in the act of following in a shotgun swing, hunting is as natural an act as drawing breath—as sipping a cool drink from the spring in the heat of cutting fuel for this fire. For a few good friends, loved ones, and me, this feral old hill farm is where we've seen things, lived moments that embraced us into the weave of a place and its planet.

When my son Aaron reached that age when you, as parent, still want to but know you no longer need to sit within arm's reach of a young hunter's rifle, he killed a deer on his own that drew us both deeper into that weave. He had climbed the high ridge south of the lake before sunup, as we had done together many times, and waited there, watching oak-timbered benches in the cold.

All morning I resisted the urge to climb up to him. Kids know when your expressed interest in whether they've seen a deer is really a screen to assure yourself they are safe. Late in the morning, I heard one shot from the ridge, the crisp crack of Aaron's .243.

The embroiled emotions sparked by a single shot from your own child's location are known only to a parent who has encouraged that youngster to hunt. First is the rush of optimistic joy, the hope that your pupil has met success and that it all happened cleanly and quick. Fast to follow, though, is that darkest unthinkable possibility, which you strangle by sheer intellectual will, and the knowledge that you taught him well. It helps, too, that you know he is cooler, more self-contained, in the woods than you were at that age.

His shot was my cue. I could go to him then without pretense. I left my own place in the hollow and climbed up across the slope, through the belt of poplar, over the thin snow toward the oaks on the crest, feeling in each step the known distance between us shrink.

I topped the last rise in the poplar woods and saw a deer lying bright and illuminate on the ground pine and the snow. It was a buck, and it lay on its left side, headed downhill away from Aaron's stand. A dark trickle of blood traced the channel of its nostril and fanned out on the snow, fading from scarlet to pink to clear ice in the span of an acorn cap. The bottomless black pool of its right eye had not yet begun to glaze. Its last tracks, sprinkled pink with blood, etched back across the flat, coming out from the oak bench where I knew Aaron was hunting. Coming up on the deer, I knew my son had killed a buck before he did, and I mulled what to do. Should I yell for him, backtrack the deer to his stand, wait?

An orange coat and hat off in the trees on the vector of the track gave me the answer. Aaron was trailing the buck, and so engrossed in the search that he hadn't seen me.

It had not been my intention to barge in at the climax, and being there, watching, held a conflict. Seeing him move along the trail, stopping to squat, survey and assess, I felt fatherly pleasure. At the same time, it felt like being an outside observer to something deeply private. The best way for the hunt to end would have been the way it began, with Aaron on his own. Tracking a shot deer can be an anxious trial for an experienced hunter, and I tried to imagine my son's thoughts. Did he fear he might not find his deer? Was he wondering how I'd react if he lost it?

I dropped back beneath the crest and waited. After a while, I heard the crunch of his boots on the snow, coming nearer, then speeding up fast. Then quiet. Finally, I heard the slick metallic sounds of an action opening and the clink of brass as he unloaded the gun. After a discreet few minutes, I climbed over the rise to where he sat in the snow next to the deer. His grin was pure and infectious, and I could feel one fixed on my own face for long minutes after.

We field-dressed the buck amid quiet, matter-of-fact conversation about its anatomy, his shot's effect, the buck's robust condition, and where from that hillside it might have ranged through its life. We sniffed at the shreds of pungent green cherry bark embedded in the burred base of its antlers. "He's been rubbing in the old field on Hans's place," we concluded.

That night, at home, we skinned him in the shed, and I showed Aaron how to fillet the backstraps, long, dense cylinders of lean muscle, away from the backbone and ribs. We stripped the silverskin membrane from the red meat, much as you would slip the skin from a filleted walleye or salmon and cut the backstraps into inch-thick butterflied steaks. Leaving the rest of the carcass to chill for boning, we took the steaks into the house and browned four of them fast on a hot iron skillet with butter and garlic.

The meat was so delicious that we ate them greedily, saying little but knowing much. Aaron had killed other deer with me at his side; this was the first when he'd been alone on the hill, yet there was no boast from him, no bravado. We extolled the meat's rich flavor and its lean wholesomeness, sharing knowing glances and nods of the head, but we sensed the meal's true significance inside the silence. This delectable meat was our most intimate approach to the hills and woods we sought to know earlier in the day through our presence there. Metabolized from acorns and maple buds, the venison bridged any divide between the white, cold quiet of the woods and ourselves. That link was what we'd coveted, though never verbalized in the preparations to hunt. When you know that a young hunter you've helped along comprehends that connection, something inside relaxes, makes an hour alone by a fire by the lake feel round and complete.

Still, here, hunts have ended well enough without the meat, yielding their own satisfaction. My daughter Colleen's first deer hunt was, perhaps, not well-timed by her dad. I have wondered since if my own zeal trumped prudence in leading her up the ridge that morning when the thermometer registered -9°, when the snow squealed under our boots, and the wind rattled treetops and stung our eyes like smoke from sodden cherry. But that was at a time before more enlightened deer management; the doe season was short (institutionalized under-harvest), and you had to go out within the brief window when you legally could.

In my defense, I had done much to make it bearable for an hour or two. I'd stuffed my pack with extra clothes, handwarmers, even a tightly rolled down sleeping bag she could huddle inside as a last resort.

Still, the cold called in accounts.

"Dad. My hands are cold," Colleen whispered. "I can't even feel them. I don't think I could even shoot."

I still believed she'd get her chance. If someone else was up and moving to pump their blood and jumped a deer nearby, it might cross this bench to seek cover in the grape and greenbriar thickets below.

"Remember when you were little; how we warmed your hands when we were sled riding?" I asked.

She nodded quickly, and I helped her pull off her gloves. I unzipped my coat and vest, pushed her pink-chilled hands inside my shirt and pressed them under my arms. The cold from her waxen flesh burned my own flesh, but her face relaxed with my warmth.

While we sat there in unlikely hunting juxtaposition, I kept watch over her left shoulder, down through the trees. Amid the grapevines beyond, I saw a flicker of movement and watched it long enough to be sure.

"Turn around slow and pick up the gun," I hissed.

The doe stepped out into open timber and started across the bench at a steady walk, maybe 50 yards below us. Colleen, now without gloves, had the rifle up across the big log we'd perched behind to blunt the wind.

As if in some cosmic choreography, the deer stopped in the one best possible spot for a shot, stark and close against the snow.

"I see it, Dad," she whispered. "The cross is right on the shoulder."

"Then go ahead."

Her icy-white finger tightened on the trigger, and I waited for the ending I had hoped for and she had earned. The deer stood still, unaware as a bluegill before a snapper's attack.

Snick!

What an odd thing to be surprised by silence. Silence is normally an ambient background, the quiet canvas upon which other sounds apply themselves. But when it is unexpected, silence is the loudest, most incongruent sound in the woods. Silence boomed.

Colleen turned her head and looked at me, asking with her eyes what had happened. Finally, I grasped it. The rifle had failed to fire. I reached over and worked the bolt. A shiny live round kicked out into the snow.

"'Shoot' again," I said.

More silence . . . ,

Snick!

The deer, somehow still unalarmed, walked off toward dense cover beyond.

I groped for explanations. Too cold? Frozen oil on the firing pin? All the theories seemed lame, and Colleen knows her dad is no gunsmith.

I gave Colleen my open-sighted Winchester, and we stayed there in the wind on the ridge until the end of light, but no more deer presented her a shot.

"Cold?" I asked her time and again.

"Yeahhh."

"Wanna quit?"

"Nope," she'd say through pursed, bluish lips.

Her first hunt had offered much—challenge, excitement, opportunity, and success. The success was there in her triumph over disappointment and her quiet endurance of conditions that beat grown men back to cars and camps by mid-morning. Something suggests to me that if you can accept the discomfort a place and an enthusiastic parent confront you with, other connections come easier from that time forth. Colleen was 13 then, my only daughter at the onset of her adolescence, and when I thought about the cold, the deer, the gun and how she'd handled it all, I felt a little better about the years ahead.

Self-discovery here goes back a long way to my own youth. In October 1971, three high school friends and I conspired to "live off the land" here for a week. The romantic urge of self-sufficiency must have been strong because, had it been exposed, our complex plot to explain our absence from home would have met immediate veto. No less noteworthy, the Pirates were playing in the World Series for the second time in our lives, and we'd opted to live in the woods rather than watch the games in a time before instant access to scores and highlights.

It was a warm and sunny autumn. We pitched a canvas wall tent on a little bluff among the poplars where our camp could not be seen from the lake, hunted and ate the big orange fox squirrels that bask in the sun on smooth gray beech bark. Some of the squirrels we took with bow and arrow, then skinned and skewered them picturesquely over the fire like "mountain men" or longhunter scouts. We tried for a pair of mallards on the lake but failed. We caught largemouth bass and broiled them over coals on frames fashioned from slippery elm twigs, lashed with their own green inner bark. After a couple of days of starchless diet, someone had the idea to concoct acorn soup, pounding the nuts on rocks, then boiling the gritty mash over the fire into a watery gray gruel. I continue to read about acorn soups and stews as a legitimate culinary possibility. And I understand now that aboriginal users of acorns leached the tannic bitterness from the seeds by immersion in streams for months, but the taste lingers yet, and I have never been moved enough to try it again.

Something else lingers too, a sense that those few days in the October sun and evening chill were a good and natural thing, a rooting of something deep, shared among friends who would rarely encounter one another again across the years, yet would be carried within each of them through time to other places, other people, and more complicated phases of life.

We need that rooting. It doesn't mean we need to stay in the same physical place, as I have done through much of my life, but we need the knowledge that we did once sense roots in the Earth and that the rooting can happen through events shared in a particular place.

* * *

My fire has burned down to ashen coals, and the smoke no longer smarts. I wash the two tenderloins I cut from inside the doe's body cavity in the lake's outflow and smear them with the Pride of Szeged Hungarian steak rub I keep in my truck in deer season. These I lay side by side, as they were in life, on the square of aluminum grill that I salvaged from a defunct toaster oven. The meat contracts a little, spits and hisses when it hits the metal. Lying there, charring, the loins suggest the size and shape of wild brook trout, a very few of which have also graced this grill. When blood begins to rise and puddle on their upper surface, I turn the meat with the point of the same knife that opened the doe to expose it. Minutes later, I lift one loin to my lips on the same tool, blowing across its surface to cool it.

The charred rind around the meat yields to a soft but dense red center. Chewing is no work at all as if the residual wild energy in this dark muscle is still bound to support and propel bone, only now it's my jawbone instead of the deer's pelvis and ribs.

The sun has slipped out around the clouds, and its rays slant down across the back of my left shoulder, elbow and hand. The warmth is immediate, balancing for the first time the released heat from within the hickory that strikes me from the opposing direction but originated, ultimately, from precisely the same source. A squadron of crows flaps and caws into the west. The wind stirs with the warming air, flaring my coals.

I finish the meat, looking all the while at the rest of the doe hanging head down from the frame, and a fleeting sense rises in me the way the warmth from the coals rises and slacks in the ambient cold. It is a sense that does not often rise through and above the layers of life's rote routines. I live 50 miles away, which is where I begin and end most days. But here, within this waning smoke, I am most at home.

Afterglow

Under moonlight, I can read my son Aaron's writing on stiff white paper—"Deerburger, PA Doe"—as we carry the last box of wrapped venison uphill to the house. Halfway across the short span from our shed-turned-butcher-shop, we cut three deer tracks that weren't there when we went down that hill earlier to bone-out, grind, and wrap meat. The depths of the tracks look ink-blue in the moonlight, and a clump of black pellets has melted its way down into the snowpack beside the biggest prints. I reach down and squeeze them just enough to gauge the timing. No warmth is left, but they aren't yet frozen; they feel like a new tube of toothpaste in the grip. It occurs to me that this pointless analysis is involuntary; it's habit. I have been hunting a lot and that's a hard thing to let go.

The deer season is over now, and we are crafting any way we can to stretch its sense of purpose and adventure out a bit longer. Butchering—making meat—is an ancient way to prolong the hunt we know won't return for another year. Now, it's our way, too, a most satisfying continuum. In justifying the time it takes to cut a deer well, I have explained the process as my personal obligation to a wild living thing whose life I took. But Kathy says I just like to be around deer for as long as possible. It feels like we are both right.

Last evening, I drove down the mountain and picked up my dad. We returned and made 30 pounds of bologna and 20 of curly-rope kielbasa—signature sausage of Western Pennsylvania's steel valleys and coal towns. We shared a workmanlike but easy evening on the cold concrete floor, our breath spewing out in white plumes against the light bulbs. I held the casings on the stuffer tube while he scooped the seasoned meat and fed it into the grinder's maw, pausing less frequently than I would need to warm a hand over the propane heater's hiss. His generation is tougher against such trifles.

The casings swelled and stiffened, and we tied off each one with a hunk of white string. Our talk was simple: "We're getting these tighter than last year." Or, "That garlic smells about right." It is straightforward, meaningful work that does not call for complex communication. As with all good and simple acts, it is the doing and the sharing that count. It's easy to imagine how it's been that way with humans around the Earth for tens of thousands of years.

When they are fully stuffed, the sausages are hefty and smooth. Stowing them in the icebox feels like the pride you get from stacking prime firewood for winter or from gazing at rows of canned tomatoes on a basement shelf.

Outside, the hides of two big does hang, salted for some later use, beneath my canoes on the rack in the yard. Each time I go out, I like to pause and look at them there and am not sure I know why. Like the meat they so recently embraced within themselves, the hanging hides evoke an older and less complex way of living. Or maybe it's just that two clean deer hides hanging beneath two battered canoes suggest that some of the time I've been granted has been well spent—something to savor in the blue light of a winter night.

Tea for Two; Flower Child

Nature, near at hand, compels us to share its manifestations with others. When the other is a beloved child, the sharing is more than the sum of parts—a mutual human experience with plant or animal, weather or place, scent, sound, or taste. Sharing nature with a child feels like you're plugging into something timeless that transcends your own mortal span. And, hopefully, it enriches hers.

My granddaughter Safari is six now. Since she could toddle, she was attracted to, then smitten by, the robust stands of bee balm that grow along the woods' edge near her swings and sliding board at our place. No wonder. Bee balm's showy scarlet flowers stood at just about her eye-level through her early years, and the tennis-ball-size blooms demand notice. Neither hummingbirds, bees, butterflies, nor a human gaze can resist them. In early summer, when visiting here, she'll inspect the sturdy growing stems for emerging blooms. This year, just before the Fourth of July, she exclaimed, "Pappy, the bee balm is coming!" By the holiday, the blooms were in spectacular display.

Safari's affiliation with bee balm even extends beyond the life of the blooms. When she was younger, she'd play imaginatively with the desiccated stems and seedheads in her sandbox. She'd strip away all but one pair of the largest opposite-arranged leaves, and with a drying stem in each hand, her child's eye saw those prominent opposite leaves beneath the spherical seedhead as "wings," and she proclaimed the plant's remains "bee balm angels." She would move the stems up and down to flap the "wings" and "fly" the angels above the other toys in her sand.

Bee balm is a native wild plant of the mint family. You can tell it's a mint by its spicy fragrance, but more assuredly by twirling a stem between your fingers. While most plants' stems are round in cross-section, the stems of members of the mint family are square. Their right angles and flat surfaces are unmistakable against the fingertips as you twirl the stem.

Once, when people came into more regular contact with plants, they gave different names to the same plant in different places for different reasons. In various places throughout its range and across time, bee balm has also been known as bergamot, horsemint, and, most notably, Oswego tea. Lore has it, and there seems every reason to trust its veracity, that Iroquois people along the Oswego River in western New York showed missionaries and fur traders how to make tea from bee balm's flowers and leaves, so the Oswego tea name, though infrequently used today, probably preceded all the others, at least among early European arrivals to North America. Certainly, Native people knew what we call bee balm by some other name in their own languages.

Bee balm grows best in partial shade on moderately moist soils. Its native range can best be characterized as "eastern Great Lakes-Appalachian." This attractive plant has been introduced to lots of places but was originally found only across a broad swath along the southern shores of Lakes Ontario and Erie, extending southwest along the Appalachians to Alabama. As a native, it's most widespread across northern and western Pennsylvania. In "Wildflowers of the Alleghenies" (1931), Joseph E. Harned states that bee balm is "Common throughout the mountains," then elaborates on setting: ". . . its beauty is greatly enhanced by an appropriately selected environment, which consists of a background of shady woods where it adds attractive interest to many a winding mountain brook."

Safari's natural, innocent attraction to the plant inspired my impulse that she and I should make a batch of bee balm tea. I knew it was a simple process that could engage a young child and hoped it would reinforce her affection for the plant that had arisen naturally out of a toddler's delight.

Late in July, after the bee balm had begun to age and decline, Safari was to spend a day at our place, which she's often done. I got everything we'd need ready in advance, then introduced the idea when she arrived. She seemed a little puzzled by the concept of tea from a flower but was eager to get started. I let her snip dozens of stems, complete with the leaves and flowerheads, and stuff them into quart canning jars. She enjoyed this part, noting that "The bee balm won't last much longer anyway, Pappy."

Wanting the entire process to happen outdoors and near the bee balm stands, we built a wood fire in our outdoor fireplace and set my three carbon-blackened coffee pots used on campouts and fishing trips on a grill over the flames. When they boiled, I helped her pour the hot water into the jars over the bee balm flowers and stems.

She was amazed at the rapid infusion of red pigment into the tea, and I thought, "This was a great idea."

We let the tea steep for about 20 minutes while we batted a Wiffle Ball around the yard. Then we strained it through coffee filters into new glass jars. The color was appealing, and the scent much like you'd expect from tea.

I believed she'd like the tea better cold than hot, so we waited longer, grazing on ripe blackberries that grow near the bee balm. When our deep-pink tea had cooled, I mixed in a little sugar to make it more pleasing to a child's palate, and we poured it over ice into glasses. This was the moment the whole effort had built toward.

She sipped, then again. A look of tentative apprehension crept over her face, and she lowered her glass. After a few moments, poignantly reluctant to disappoint her mentor in tea-making, she said meekly, "Pappy, I, I don't like it."

I couldn't blame her. Bee balm tea has an "adult" floral taste that needs to be acquired to enjoy. After all, does commercial "store-bought" tea actually "taste good?" Or is it the hot brace of caffeine that we anticipate and learn to like? Harned called bee balm's fragrance, arising from the same resinous oils that infuse the tea, "redolent, with a so-called Balm or Bergamot odor."

Harned's reference to "Bergamot" was to the Bergamot orange, a fragrant citrus fruit with qualities of lemon and orange. Its spicy scent is close to that of bee balm and other mints of the Genus *Monarda*. A near relative to bee balm is still known as bergamot today. It's similar to bee balm in every way except that the flowers are lavender in color, the leaves and stems are less robust, and it prefers drier, sunnier locations.

Tea Life, a website devoted to herbal teas made from wild and cultivated plants, describes bee balm's taste as an "... herbal flavor that is a combination of mint, basil and even oregano." That report comes as close to the taste as anything I could produce. We saved all the jars, and I find I enjoy the tea better served hot.

Whatever your reaction to bee balm tea's taste, it's believed to have a wide range of medicinal and therapeutic attributes. Indians who drank the tea for centuries are said to have used it to relieve coughs, sore throats, and various stomach ailments.

Modern herbalists cite evidence that bee balm has antiseptic properties and makes an effective and pleasant tasting, as opposed to some commercial brands, mouthwash.

Perhaps I was over-ambitious in envisioning my granddaughter would like wild tea made from the brilliant red flowers she anticipates every summer and devises into toys. But I still see the experiment as successful. Knowing her, I would not be surprised if, when she's older, she suggests we try it again. And I'm certain the experience deepened her already developing sense that connections to the natural world are available all around us, especially when one employs curiosity, innovation, and a little effort. If I'm honest, though, I'm most pleased by the possibility that a simple exercise, close to home between the woods and the fireplace, will later evoke memories of her grandfather whenever she encounters those vivid red blooms throughout her life.

Memoirs of a Quehanna Chief

"Wanted: Young men, college graduates, comfortable outdoors."
—*Uniontown Evening Standard*

I was enthralled by this classified ad that appeared in late March 1976. To work in some way conserving the outdoors where I'd grown up fishing, hunting and foraging wild plants was how I'd always envisioned my life. But what job could this be?

The ad's timing was ironic. I'd just returned home from two futile months couch-surfing off friends of friends in Washington, D. C. Buoyed by a new degree in an oddly cobbled major that Penn State called "Environmental Resource Management," I'd made cold-call visits to the National Park Service, U.S. Forest Service, U. S. Fish and Wildlife Service and any other "service" whose title sounded as if it might offer "outdoor" work in wild places. When I walked into federal headquarters asking for a job, the receptionists' stares were blank. Thankfully, I had a lot to learn about a government employment search because that help-wanted ad led to the most demanding and memorable work of my life.

I called the number and learned that Pressley Ridge Wilderness School, near Ohiopyle, had placed the ad. I'd hunted grouse and fished for trout around Ohiopyle, yet I'd never heard of the place. The last half-mile of the drive to my interview made me glad for my 1969 Bronco's four-wheel-drive, and I felt more at home than in any stuffy office I'd crashed in D.C. That comfort, though, was short-lived. The first sight to confront me was a tall adolescent boy cavorting on the roof of a rustic but official-looking building, tearing up shingles and flipping them, like Frisbees, to a delighted knot of boys below. Two taller and bearded young men were trying to restore order.

Pressley Ridge Camp, as it was sometimes called, was a therapeutic outdoor program for "emotionally disturbed" adolescent boys. I learned that the job offered was teacher-counselor and that my lack of formal training in psychology or childcare was not considered an obstacle. My interests and skills in the outdoors, I was told, would fit well into the school's way of working with troubled kids. Each counselor lived with a group of ten boys and one counselor-partner in tents on the school's "campus." Four groups were already living there, widely spread across 1,200 acres of boulder-strewn woods. If hired, my partner and I would nurture ten new boys yet to be enrolled, filling out the program's complement of five resident groups.

When Director Jim Doncaster called later and offered me the job, I was conflicted. I wouldn't be working to protect wildlife or conserve forests, as I'd imagined my career, but I'd be out in the woods every day. I accepted, and after a couple of weeks camping with experienced counselors and their groups, my new partner Terry Dunkle, a trained childcare worker from Pittsburgh, and I met the boys with whom we'd live in the woods.

Most were from tough Pittsburgh neighborhoods, but some came out of rough rural parts of surrounding counties. All were behaviorally challenged in some way, most on the wrong side of the law. Many had no secure family foundation.

Nothing revealed the challenges these boys faced like their "home-stays." At six-week intervals, we drove them home for brief visits with whatever family they had. One boy, Hank, was a chronic bed-wetter, which brought on considerable scorn. Terry and I tried hard to help him overcome the humiliating habit, waking him at night then walking the trail to the latrine through all kinds of weather. Hank was morose and quiet the first time we arrived at his mother's dank apartment for home-stay, where a suffocating stench enveloped us at the door. Nestled deep within a bulky recliner, Hank's mom apologized for the odor but confided that since she could not muster the motivation to get up and walk to the bathroom, she voided her bladder there in her chair.

Pressley's staff arranged a family conference for another boy from a declining coal patch in Somerset County. His mother arrived for the meeting with a male companion, and as we discussed her son's progress, she and her date engaged in an intense make-out session in the crowded room with her son in attendance. The camp director aborted the session. I couldn't imagine how a young boy processed such a thing, but things like this explained some of their behavior. Fathers were not in the picture for most of the boys.

Another window into their backgrounds was "pow-wow," convened by each group around their fire every night before bed. At pow-wow, boys spoke openly about anything they wished that dealt with their progress in camp or their hopes for the future. Pow-wow was always enlightening, sometimes heartwarming, and often sobering. Encircled, their faces flamelit, the boys shared their home lives or lack thereof. I learned for the first time how fortunate I'd been.

In camp, the group took the place of family. Groups worked, cooked, ate, slept, and planned their week ahead as a unit. Group progress and comfort depended on every member's input. Ours was among camp's older groups, age 15-17. Pressley Ridge encouraged adoption of Native American tribal titles, place names or cultural icons for the names of groups, and boys referred to their teacher-counselors as "chiefs." After weighing several suggestions, the boys chose "Quehanna" as our group's name. In my understanding, the word is of Algonquian origin, translating roughly to "Camping place near a stream," fitting ours well.

Quehanna lived in a cluster of tents beside Long Hollow Run, near a flat spot between boulders where we would build ourselves a cabin. We needed to get the cabin finished before winter hit Laurel Ridge, but constructing a livable structure working with boys who had rarely cooperated with anyone on any endeavor was a daunting task. Yet, it presented just the kind of group challenge and reliance on one another that brought out ways to employ each boy's skills, and progress quickened as autumn approached. That cabin, built by Quehanna in the summer of 1976, remained in use throughout the life of the Pressley Ridge program. Later groups built lighter shelters of canvas lashed to logs every spring for summer use, then dismantled them each fall before moving into the cabin so that all groups passing through the program provided shelter for themselves.

We worked on the cabin almost daily, cut firewood (no chainsaws), dug the latrine and laid a gravity-aided water line from a spring higher on the ridge. We cooked at our campsite three days each week and ate common meals in the dining hall the rest. Say what you will about assigning adjudicated boys to the woods with sharp tools in their reach, but camp life offered them something I believe is missing from the lives of nearly all modern American youth—tasks simple enough for a boy to complete yet also important to the group's welfare and comfort. There's therapy in that.

Because of my own affinity for outdoor life, I suppose my most vivid remembrances surround the boys' blossoming ease in what was initially to them an alien place. Some could mimic bird calls—jays, thrushes or ovenbirds among them. Weather predictions soon came from informed experience, and boys taught newcomers to pluck teaberries along the trail for snacks. "Tastes just like gum," they'd proclaim. Quehanna boys learned to know all the trees of the Alleghenies—which trees' wood was useful as fuel, which split readily, and which could last as coals in the cabin's wood-stove, quick to rekindle at wake-up, through nights when our boots froze to the floor.

Always, I will remember the first time a grin replaced one boy's habitual scowl. His name was Teddy, and he'd grown up in Pittsburgh's Garfield district. Teddy was tall, athletic and quick to anger, but he had a sensitive side when something cut through his steely façade. We were cutting wood with bow saws. It was hot, and I bent to slurp cupped handfuls from the clear cold spring where Teddy had refused for weeks to drink because "That's dirty, man." But this time, in the July heat, he relented. He stretched his long frame on the ferns and slaked deep. When he rose, his face was dewy, a cool tautness to his dark skin, and his smile flashed wide. "Y'all is makin' me into a mountain man!"

Sometime later, Teddy and I paddled a canoe among snags of flooded timber on Cranberry Glade Lake. As we drifted close to one snag, a hole in its trunk at eye-level filled up with metallic-green feathers, and a tree swallow flashed away over the lake. We sculled in close, and Teddy peered inside the cavity, leaning the canoe to starboard. I saw his jaw drop and his grip on the snag melt to a caress. Turning back toward me, he could not contain a child-like awe through the bluster he normally bore. Inside, he'd seen the swallow's nest crammed with nestlings, open-mouthed and reaching. I think he perceived their vulnerability amid a hard indifferent world like the one he'd known himself.

I think about Teddy more often than any other boy I knew there. For months after the tree swallow sighting, Teddy walked the trails to dining hall and showers with his long arm slung around my neck, leaning his weight into my stride. But once, after I'd slighted him in some way I didn't suspect, he wheeled around in the path and sucker-punched me hard in the face. I heard an internal "crunch," blood gushed from my nose and lips, and, in case you have never absorbed such a blow, you really do see stars.

Such violence wasn't routine, but as with any group of boys that age, fights sometimes happened, and rebellious campers did chafe at their chiefs' authority. But mostly, the groups functioned as cooperating quasi-families, as Pressley's treatment model envisioned.

Sometimes there was poignant tenderness that I would never have experienced in any other way. Late in my tenure at Pressley, I was promoted to "roving counselor." Rovers were not assigned to a group but circulated around camp, offering veteran insight and helping chiefs who were struggling.

In this role, I spent some time with the camp's youngest group, in which twin brothers Duayne and Dave were enrolled. Both were slight and shy, small for their age. And like many of the black campers, each carried a "pick" in a hip pocket for grooming the Afro hairstyles then popular. Sometimes, in the evening, before the boys quieted down to bed and while the woodstove exuded coveted heat, Duayne and Dave would sit on rough wooden benches next to one of their chiefs and me, pull out their picks, and comb our beards.

We never asked them why they did this, and we never felt justified in discouraging such an innocent outreach toward human warmth. During the day, the twins could be as quick to throw a rock in anger or sneer out a curse as any of the others. But when they stroked their picks through our ragged beards, it seemed the boys had surrendered to a basic craving to be tactilely close to an adult mentor. I don't recall their family history, what kind of relationship they had with their father, or if they even knew him.

I only know that it was humbling to sense their quiet satisfaction in this simple act of affection.

The other boys never mocked Duayne or Dave for what in any other setting would have appeared an unthinkable breach of norm. I believe the others understood the twins' need and maybe let the beard-combing stand for their own unexpressed longing for adult bonds.

Learning through experience was at the core of the camp model. One evening in early November of that first year, we cooked supper at our Quehanna camp. We had nearly completed our cabin, which, though still crude in appearance, was dry and warm—warm if the boy whose turn it was got up in the night to feed the stove (a simple but important task, openly lauded by the group when accomplished). Chief Terry and I looked forward to a placid evening around the hearth, but some insult incited a melee, and chaos reigned until past the hour we were normally in our bags, lanterns extinguished.

Outside, around the fire where we'd eaten, all the cooking gear lay strewn like the leaves of late autumn. Whichever boy had dishwashing duty had been embroiled in the strife like everyone else, and the chore went undone (This was unusual. The boys' pride in a clean camp was impressive and nearly universal). When calm finally reigned, we chiefs had no energy or patience left for any task beyond getting the boys into bed.

That night, 12 inches of dense wet snow, the first of the season, fell across Laurel Ridge. Sleep had soothed all tension, but no utensils for cooking or eating could be found beneath the snow. Still, the boys could always get a fire going, another source of pride among them. So, we sat around that fire, the 12 of us, passing around two big cans of tepid pork and beans bashed open with an ax and the one dubious spoon someone found by their bunk. No one in our somber circle could escape the truth that undesirable consequences follow irresponsible impulses.

I think that one of the things boys truly liked about life at Pressley Ridge Wilderness School was that it carried a sense of mild adventure. Frank, a boy known to the group for his habitual lying, led our single-file return one summer morning after breakfast. Trailing everyone, I couldn't see Frank ahead, but his agitated voice pierced the screening laurel.

"Snake! Chief Ben, there's a snake up here!" Frank squealed

Everyone assumed the outburst was one of Frank's untruths. Yet, something in his alarm said he'd been too shocked to concoct a tale.

"Chief! Get up here now," Frank yelled. "Rattlesnake!"

I shouldered along the line and heard it before I reached his side—that angry, chitinous buzz. The group pressed in around Frank and me in concentric rings. At our center, in the trail, a large yellow-phase timber rattlesnake writhed in tense coils, its broad head poised. The velvety-black tail stood erect among arcs of keel-scaled muscle, swaying back and forth while the terminal rattle blurred with motion. Jagged black chevrons slashed across its sulfur hide.

I found a suitable stick and pinned the head, then grasped the neck close behind the skull and picked the snake up, cradling its heft with my left hand and forearm. The boys' hooted exclamations sounded far away, but they pressed nearer.

At Pressley Ridge Camp, boys were encouraged to share their wildlife encounters in the dining hall at evening meal. Revealing some unique observation was a daily aspiration for groups. Quehanna kept its rattlesnake in the shade in a cleaned plastic trash barrel until supper, when the boys had the honor of standing before the entire camp, recounting the capture, climaxed by a showing of the reptile to the enthralled assembly.

The next day, with the snake in a knotted pillowcase, our group hiked to a remote ledge on the tract's perimeter, where we released it unharmed in the morning sun. The rattler capture was, for me, a happenstance way to win a bit of the boys' regard, which helped our relationships in various ways. At pow-wow, the event wrought an earnest discussion about the import of being believed when one spoke. Quehanna signed *Peterson's Field Guide to Reptiles and Amphibians* out of the camp library, and native reptiles were a topic in the boys' talk for the rest of that summer.

Less dramatic adventures brought the boys intimate contact with other wild creatures. Because our campsite crowded a hemlock-shrouded mountain run, I kept a back-packable, 5-piece fly rod in my tent. When we took "siesta" at midday, meant for napping, reading, or quiet time, some of the group would accompany me to the stream. Stealth is key in such fishing but difficult for boys of that raucous age. Still, they grasped its import once they understood wild trout.

They gaped the first time I lifted a native brook trout from its emerald pool, dazzled by a new sense of what a fish from western Pennsylvania woods could look like. And with coaching, they, too, pulled up wriggling trout, speckled and smooth, from that step-across run. Like Teddy and his epiphany at the spring, those fishing sessions dominate my thoughts about camp even now. It would be crass to pretend such brief idylls changed the boys' lives in any way; their futures were all uphill. But I will say that, for a moment, when a boy felt that courageous tug from beneath some hemlock root, his demons eased, and a reckless grin consumed his face.

I will always treasure the pride I felt in association with Pressley Ridge professionals. I admired my co-workers and my supervisors there and felt my own self-esteem boosted, knowing they considered me a peer. Clark Luster, then executive director over all Pressley Ridge programs, often visited camp, and once he referred to us chiefs as his "blue-jeaned psychologists." The honor I felt in that impromptu moniker is hard now to put into words, but I can still sense its impact.

Working with difficult boys in the woods instilled bonds of camaraderie among chiefs that I have never known equaled in a workplace since. I offer here a sense of this bonding through an incident you may find hard to believe happened in an enlightened university town in 1976, but it did.

During one of the boys' longer "home-stays," our entire staff rode the camp bus to in-service training at Tremont Environmental Education Center, inside Great Smoky Mountains National Park, which stressed the very aspects of therapeutic camping that I took to naturally. I loved the trip for all kinds of reasons, and when the sessions were complete, we drove that bus into downtown Knoxville for an evening of social diversion, cold beers and dancing with some female students from the University of Tennessee. When we left the last bar, a mob of young fellows about our age followed us and surrounded the bus. Shouting slurs and pounding on the windows, they demanded that we turn over to them one of our two black chiefs, or else our bus wasn't moving. They got more than they bargained for. Toned by wood-cutting and cabin-raising, and seasoned to confrontation, we all piled off among them at once. When we smugly re-took our seats, our bus was free to roll, and that mob slunk away with a new regard for the Yankees they'd jeered.

I don't know why the wilderness school closed. When the last boys walked the last trail there, I had long moved on to other things, marriage among them, which was not compatible with the job's residential demands. Based solely on my layman's observations, group work in the woods had seemed a fiscally efficient and effective way of working with certain kids, thoughtfully chosen for Pressley's "open" program, and I'm sure the decision to shut down the camp was not made lightly. Viewed now in hindsight from near the quarter-mark of the 21st century, I sense that the whole therapeutic camping concept has fallen out of favor among the childcare profession nationwide, plagued, I'd wager, by societal hyper-paranoia about insect bites, sun exposure, natural darkness, isolation from the internet, and our modern incomprehensibility of living without central air.

It is hard for me to fathom that the boys I came to know best at Pressley Ridge Wilderness School would all be in their late-50s now, graying, with grandkids, perhaps, a part of their lives. I see them instead frozen, forever young, looking backward through my own life lens as if they'd been immutable features of that mountain landscape, like the boulders outside the cabin we built before winter's snow. They were not immutable, of course. They were boys maturing to men, and I hope so deeply that some bright path opened to each.

About the Author

Ben Moyer's writing on nature, outdoors, and conservation issues appears in numerous regional and national publications including Northern Appalachia Review and Pittsburgh Quarterly magazine. In 2019, the Outdoor Writers Association of America honored Moyer with its Excellence in Craft Award, which recognizes an outstanding lifetime body of work. His writing has also garnered numerous awards from the Pennsylvania Outdoor Writers Association and the Mason-Dixon Outdoor Writers Association. Moyer strives to convey the value of personal affiliation with place, in his case Northern Appalachia, while interpreting scientific concepts and the region's natural history through creative prose.

In addition to his writing, Moyer is president of the Chestnut Ridge Chapter of Trout Unlimited, which works to protect, improve, and restore wild trout streams in the Laurel Highlands region of southwestern Pennsylvania. He writes and lives in Fayette County, Pennsylvania, with his wife Kathy.

www.ingramcontent.com/pod-product-compliance
Lightning Source LLC
Chambersburg PA
CBHW031434270326
41930CB00007B/707